JN268323

耳できいて、こんなに使える最強英語173

イディオム・ハンドブック

Helen Kalkstein Fragiadakis 著
柳浦 恭 訳

NEWBURY HOUSE
HEINLE & HEINLE

松柏社

耳できいて、こんなに使える 最強英語イディオム・ハンドブック173

Helen Kalkstein Fragiadakis 著
柳浦 恭 訳

NEWBURY HOUSE
HEINLE & HEINLE

松柏社

ALL CLEAR! —Idioms in Context
Copyright © 1993 by Heinle & Heinle Publishers
This authorized adaptation published by Newbury House 2003

ISBN4-7754-0042-8

ALL RIGHTS RESERVED. No part of this book may be reproduced or transmitted in any form or by any means, electronic or mechanical, including photocopying, recording, or any information storage and retrieval system, without permission, in writing, from the Publisher.

THOMSON™ LEARNING Thomson Learning logo is a trademark under license.

Printed in Japan

まえがき

　本書は高校初級程度の英語力を前提として、日本人の学習者にアメリカ英語の口語表現を紹介することを目的としています。扱われているイディオムや決まり文句は、英語を母国語とする人達の会話で頻繁に用いられているものばかりです。これらを本当に使いこなせるようになれば、会話はぐっと生き生きしたものになるでしょう。

　まず冒頭のDialogueでは自然な会話の形でイディオムや決まり文句が導入され、次にこれらの言い回しと類似表現が短い会話の中で与えられており、より理解を深めることができるように配慮されています。会話の部分はスポーツのイメージ・トレーニングのように、具体的な場面を心に描きながら結果として暗記するぐらいまで音読することをお勧めします。お友達とペアで練習してもいいでしょう。そして最後は仕上げにexercisesで理解をチェックしてください。

　本書が読者の皆さんのお役に立てれば幸いです。

2003年3月吉日

訳者

C·O·N·T·E·N·T·S

Lesson **1** Cold Feet（ビビる） 1

Lesson **2** Guess Who?（誰だと思う？） 21

Lesson **3** Please Leave a Message After You Hear the Beep（発信音の後でメッセージをどうぞ） 35

Lesson **4** In Bad Shape（調子が悪い） 57

Lesson **5** Are We Couch Potatoes?（僕たちってカウチ・ポテト族？） 75

Lesson **6** Forgetting a Date（デートをすっぽかす） 99

Lesson **7** For Here or to Go?（こちらでお召し上がりですか、お持ち帰りですか？） 113

Lesson **8** How About Going to a Movie?（映画に行くのはどう？） 139

Lesson **9** Pulling an All-Nighter（徹夜で勉強する） .155

Lesson **10** Sold Out（売り切れ） 175

Lesson **11** Don't Throw it Away—Recycle!（捨てないで。リサイクル！） 193

Lesson **12** Let's Make a Toast（乾杯しよう） 223

Cold Feet

ビビる

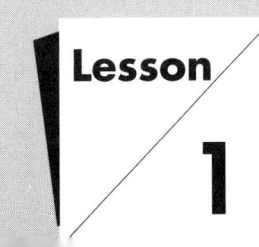

Lesson 1

D·I·A·L·O·G·U·E

ELLEN: Can you believe it? Your wedding is in two weeks!

JANA: And I think I'm **getting cold feet**.

ELLEN: Why? What are you afraid of? Rick's a great guy.

JANA: I know, but maybe we should wait. We **can't** even **afford to** buy furniture!

ELLEN: So, it's money that's making you **have second thoughts. Deep down** you really want to **get married**. I **can tell** by your face—you really love him.

JANA: Ellen, sometimes I think you can **read my mind**.

エレン: 信じられる? あなたたちの結婚式まであと2週間よ!

ジャーナ: 何かちょっと怖くなってきたわ。

エレン: どうして? リックはすばらしい人じゃない。

ジャーナ: そりゃそうだけど、もう少し待ったほうがいい気もするの。まだ家具だって揃えられないわけだし。

エレン: じゃあお金のことが原因で気が変わったということなのかしら。でも本当はあなたは彼と結婚したいのよ。顔にちゃんとそう書いてあるもの。彼のこと本当に愛してるのよ。

ジャーナ: エレン、あなたって私のことなんでも分かるのね。

D·I·A·L·O·G·U·E

RICK: Tim, can I ask you a question?

TIM: **Shoot**!

RICK: Do you think I'm ready to get married?

TIM: That's a strange question. Are you **getting cold feet**?

RICK: I guess you could say that. I was thinking, you know, marriage is **for good**, and I don't want to make a mistake. There are so many divorces these days and . . . my parents are divorced, you know. **History repeats itself** a lot and . . .

TIM : **Are** you **through**? Do you have any more reasons why you shouldn't marry Jana?

RICK: But I'm **dying to** marry her.

TIM: Do you want my advice? You and Jana **have a lot in common**. You're perfect for each other. So **cut out** all this nonsense and don't **be** so **chicken**. If you **wind up without** Jana, you'll be sorry.

リック: テイム、ちょっと聞いてもいいかい?

テイム: もちろん!

リック: 僕はもう結婚してもいいと思うかい?

テイム: 変なことを言いだすね。おじけづいたかな?

リック: そうかもしれない。ちょっと考えてたんだけど、ほら、いったん結婚したらそれまでだろ? 失敗はしたくないじゃないか。近頃は離婚も多いし...それに僕の両親も離婚してるから。よく歴史は繰り返すって言うし...

テイム: 言いたいことはそれだけ? ほかにもジャーナと結婚してはいけない理由がまだあるかな?

リック: でも彼女とはどうしても結婚したいんだ。

テイム: 僕の意見が聞きたいかい? 君とジャーナは似てるところが多いし、お互いに最高の組み合わせだと思うよ。だからくだらない事を言ってビビってたらだめだよ。もしジャーナと一緒になれないで終わったらきっと後悔すると思う。

．．．

➼ 1. **Can you believe it?** it は次の文の内容をさす。
   Your wedding is in two weeks! in は通常未来に使って「時間の経過」を表す。*cf. He will come back in a week.*

19. **I guess you could say that.** that は相手の発言内容をさす。

Cold Feet • 5

1 get/have cold feet

おじけづく、ビビる

- **A:** Your new job starts soon, doesn't it?
- **B:** Uh-huh, but the problem is, I'm **getting cold feet** and thinking that I should call them and tell them to look for someone else.

- A: 君の新しい仕事、もうすぐ始まるね。
- B: うん。でもね、何か少し**怖くなってきた**みたいなんだ。電話でもして誰か別の人を探すように言ったほうがいいかと思って。

- **A:** Didn't they get married?
- **B:** No. At the last minute, she **got cold feet** and canceled the wedding.

- A: ふたりは結婚しなかったの?
- B: うん。最後の土壇場で彼女のほうが**ためらって**式を取り消したんだ。

→ the problem is,「困ったことはね」の意味で、類似表現にはthe fact is, the point is, などがある。

2 can/can't afford (to do)...

～する(金銭的)余裕がある／ない

- **A:** I didn't know you had a job.
- **B:** Well, I **can't afford to** go to school full-time. So I work and go to school part-time.

- A: あなたが働いていたなんて知らなかった。
- B: ええ、学校だけに専念する**っていうわけにはいかなかった**の。だから働きながら学校に通っているのよ。

6 • Lesson 1

A: I thought you were going to buy a new car.
B: I wanted to, but I **couldn't afford** one. I had to get a used car, but it's OK.

A: That video camera is so expensive!
B: Don't worry. I **can afford** it.

A: 新車を買うかと思ってたのに。
B: そうしたかったんだけど、**予算の都合で中古にしたん**だ。でもそう悪くないよ。

A: あのビデオ・カメラ、すごく高いわ。
B: 心配するなよ。**何とかなる**って。

3 have second thoughts
考え直す、気が変わる

A: I'll buy it.
B: Are you sure? No **second thoughts**?
A: **No second thoughts**. Here's my check.

A: What do you think of the new guy?
B: I'm afraid I'm **having second thoughts** about him. At first, I was sure he was right for the job, but now I'm not so sure. His work isn't as good as I expected.

A: それください。
B: 本当ですか？ 後で**考え直**されることはないですか？
A: 大丈夫。じゃこれ小切手です。

A: 今度の新人、どう思う？
B: ちょっとどうかなって**思い直してる**ところだよ。最初は仕事にうってつけの人だと思ったけど、今はちょっとね。仕事っぷりも思ったほどよくないし。

Cold Feet • 7

4 deep down

心の底では、本心では

A: I told them that I wanted to fly, but **deep down** I'd really like to drive.
B: Why?
A: I've never told anyone this before, but I'm afraid of flying.

A: Look at how they are all smiling at each other. But **deep down** they really don't like each other.
B: How do you know?
A: Trust me. I know.

A: あの人達には飛行機で行きたいって言ったんだけど、**本当のことを言うと**車の方がいいの。
B: どうして？
A: 今まで誰にも言ったことがないんだけど、飛行機って苦手なの。

A: ごらん。あのふたり、ニコニコしてるでしょ。でもね、**本当は**お互いに相手が嫌いなのさ。
B: どうして分かるの？
A: どうしてもさ。僕には分かるんだ。

5 get/be married (to)
結婚する／している

A: When are you **getting married**?
B: In a month or two.

A: 君たちいつ**結婚する**の?
B: ひと月かふた月したら。

A: They're married?
B: Yup (yes). They **got married** last year.

A: ふたりは**結婚して**るの?
B: うん。去年**結婚した**んだ。

A: Did you know that Rick **is married to** Jana?
B: That's great.

A: リックがジャーナと**結婚し**てるって知ってた?
B: そりゃすばらしい。

6 can/can't tell (by)
(〜で)分かる／分からない

A: **Can** you **tell** that I was crying? Are my eyes red?
B: No, I **can't tell**. No one will notice, so don't worry.

A: 私が泣いていたって**分かる**? 目が赤くなってるかな?
B: いいや、**分からない**よ。誰にも気づかれないから心配するなよ。

A: There's a new driver in front of us.
B: How do you know?
A: I **can tell by** the way he's sitting, and how slowly he's driving.

A: 運転手さんまだ新人だね。
B: どうして**分かる**の。
A: 座り方とかゆっくりした走り方**で分かる**よ。

Cold Feet • 9

7 read *someone's* mind

他人の心を読む

A: This party isn't very exciting. You want to go home, don't you?

B: Are you **reading my mind**?

A: You knew I didn't want to fly. Why didn't we drive?

B: How could I know that you didn't want to fly? Do you think I can **read your mind**?

A: このパーティあんまり面白くないね。家へ帰りたいだろ。

B: 私の気持ちが分かるの?

A: 私が飛行機は嫌だって知ってたくせに。どうして車にしなかったの?

B: そんなこと分かるわけないだろ。僕に**他人の心が読める**とでも思ってるわけ?

8 Shoot!

いいとも！

A: There's something that I've been wanting to ask you.
B: Shoot !
A: How old are you?

A: Can I ask you a question?
B: Sure. **Shoot!**

A: あなたにちょっと聞いてみたいと思っていたことがあるんだけど。
B: いいよ！
A: 年はいくつなの？

A: 聞きたいことがあるんだけど。
B: いいとも！

➜ 非常にくだけた表現なので普通はGo ahead. と言うほうが無難。

9 for good

永遠に、ずっと

A: Our marriage is over **for good**. I don't want to talk about it.
B: But you have to talk. This is important.

A: I just got a letter from my son—finally.
B: Any news?
A: Yeah—big news. He's coming home **for good**. You know—he's been traveling for over two years?

A: わたしたちの結婚はこれで**永遠に**おしまいね。もう何も話すことはないわ。
B: でも話さなきゃ。大切なことだよ。

A: やっと息子から手紙が来たよ。
B: 何かあったの？
A: あったとも。**これを最後に**家に帰ってくるみたいだ。この２年間ずっと旅に出ていただろう？

Cold Feet • 11

10 history repeats itself
歴史は繰り返す

A: I hope there won't be another war.
B: So do I. We never seem to learn from the mistakes of the past so **history** always **repeats itself**. It's crazy.

A: また戦争がなければいいんだけど。
B: そうだね。僕らはどうやら過去の過ちから学ぶことができないから同じことが繰り返されるんだよね。馬鹿げてるよ。

11 be through (with)
(何かが)済んでいる

A: Can you help me?
B: Sure. I'll **be through** in a second.

A: ちょっと手伝って。
B: いいよ。もうすぐ手があくから。

A: When we'**re through with** our homework, do you want to take a walk?
B: That sounds like a great idea. I need to get out for a little while.

A: 宿題が終わったら散歩でも行かないか。
B: そりゃいいね。少し外に出たいと思ってたところだ。

➜ 何か能動的に行っていた行為について用いる。たとえば映画が終わったときにI'm finished with the movie.とは言えない。動詞を用いる場合は〜ingの形にする。
cf. When I'm through (with) doing the dishes, I'll take a shower.
(お皿を洗い終ったらシャワーを浴びましょう。)

12 be dying to do...
〜したくてたまらない

A: That new movie is finally here. I**'m dying to** see it. Want to come?
B: What's it about?

A: あの新作映画がついに封切りよ。どうしても見なくっちゃ。一緒に来る?
B: どんな映画?

A: Why are you going home so early?
B: I**'m dying to** get the mail. I'm expecting something kind of special.

A: 何でそんなに急いで家に帰るの?
B: 郵便が待ちどうしくって。ちょっと特別なのが来るの。

➻ かなり大げさな表現で、くだけた会話に用いる。普通は really want to do くらいでよい。

❖ **be dying of thirst/ be dying of hunger** 「喉が乾いて／お腹がすいて死にそう」

A: It's so hot and I**'m dying of thirst**. Let's stop and get a drink.
B: I haven't eaten since this morning and I**'m dying of hunger**.

A: 暑いよ! のどが渇いて死にそうだ。ちょっと休んで何か飲もう。
B: 朝から何も食べてないんだ。おなかがへって死にそうだ。

13 have a lot/nothing in common

趣味や嗜好が共通している／いない

A: Let's introduce Marie to Tom. I think they'd like each other.

B: Great idea. They **have a lot in common**, don't you think?

A: マリーをトムに紹介しようよ。お互い気が合うと思うな。

B: そりゃいいね。ふたりは**共通点が多い**と思わないかい？

A: Let's introduce Fran to Andrew. I think they'd like each other.

B: I don't think so. They **have nothing in common** (with each other). I'm surprised that you thought they'd like each other. I think we should introduce Andrew to Valerie.

A: フランをアンドリューに紹介しようよ。お互い気にいると思う。

B: それはどうかなあ。**似てるところが全然ないし**、君がそんなこと言い出すなんて驚きだよ。それよりアンドリューをバレリに紹介しよう。

14 cut out *something*

～をやめる

A: Hey—**cut out** all that noise in there!

B: Too bad! Close the door.

A: おーい。そのうるさいのやめてくれ。

B: そりゃおあいにくさま。ドアを閉めてよ。

A: You'd better **cut out** smoking because it is really bad for you.
B: You're right. Anyway, there aren't many places left where it's legal to smoke.

A: 煙草は**止めた**ほうがいいね。本当に体に悪いよ。
B: そうですよね。それにどっちみち煙草を吸ってもいい場所なんてもうそんなに残ってないし。

➨ くだけた表現。最初の会話は家族同士、次の会話は友達同士か医者と患者との間のものと思われる。通常は stop, refrain from doing を使う。

15 be chicken/be (a) chicken
こわがる／臆病者

A: Jump! Come on—you can do it.
B: No, I'm too **chicken**. It's too far and I know I'll fall.

A: 跳ぶのよ！ほら、できるんだから。
B: だめだよ。こわくって。こんなにあったら落ちちゃうよ。

A: Go tell him!
B: Ssh! No. I'**m a chicken**. You tell him.

A: 彼に言いに行きなさい。
B: だめだあ。こわいよ。君が言って。

A: Did you tell him?
B: No, I **chickened out**.

A: 彼に言った？
B: ううん。ビビッちゃった。

➨ ライオンが「勇気」を表すように、ニワトリには「小心・臆病」のイメージがある。子供が仲間に何か挑発してやらせるときに用いる表現だが、大人もくだけた会話で用いることがある。また、英語で「腰抜け」は week-kneed という。怖くなるとヒザがガクガクしてくるため。

16 wind up with/without ...

終わる

A: If you don't take better care of yourself, you'll **wind up with** a cold.
B: All right. I'll take my jacket.

A: もっと体を大事にしないとカゼひいちゃうよ(最後にはカゼをひいて終わる)。
B: そうだね。上着を着て行こう。

A: They gambled all their money and **wound up without** a cent.
B: All their money?

A: あの人達ギャンブルでお金を全部すって一文なしだよ(最後には1セントもなくなって終わる)。
B: 全部?

➻ 「結局のところ望ましくない結果に終わる」というニュアンスで用いられることが多い。

❖ wind up —ing 「結局〜になる」

A: If we don't make a decision soon. we'll **wind up going** nowhere.
B: Why don't we just go to the beach?

A: 早く決めないと結局どこにも行けなくなるよ。
B: 海でも行けばいいじゃない。

e·x·e·r·c·i·s·e·s

1 テープ(CD)を聴いて、次のダイアローグの空欄に適当な語句を書き入れてみましょう。

TIM: Still have (1)_____?
RICK: No. And I (2)_____ either. I feel great.
TIM: I (3)_____. You look really happy. So does Jana.
RICK: Where is she? Did you see her?
TIM: Oh, yeah. But you can't until the ceremony.
RICK: That's a crazy superstition. Show me where she is. I (4)_____ see her.
TIM: Oh, no. Her mother would be really mad. She told me that on the day people (5)_____, they shouldn't see each other 'til the ceremony.
RICK: I don't think that Jana's mother and I (6)_____. But (7)_____, I really like her. I hope she likes me.
TIM: I'm sure she does. She was just saying that when she's (8)_____ helping Jana, she'll come down and look for you to see how you're doing. How are you doing?
RICK: That's a good question. What time is it?

Cold Feet • 17

e·x·e·r·c·i·s·e·s

2 次の 1〜17 の文に対する返答として適当なものを 19 ページの a〜q より選んでみましょう。

_____ 1. Can I ask you a question?
_____ 2. Let's watch TV.
_____ 3. He has two cars and a boat and he works in a fast food restaurant.
_____ 4. I'm dying of thirst.
_____ 5. I'm telling them what you told me.
_____ 6. I thought you were going to make a speech in front of all the teachers.
_____ 7. Listen—I've got some interesting news for you.
_____ 8. Are they laughing or crying?
_____ 9. Let me try to read your mind. You are thinking about breaking up.
_____ 10. What are you doing here? I thought you'd be away by now.
_____ 11. All right, I'll do it.
_____ 12. What is your marital status?
_____ 13. I'm not staying here for good. I want to see the world.
_____ 14. The same thing happened a hundred years ago.
_____ 15. I like music, dancing, sports and reading.
_____ 16. I'm sorry I'm so chicken, but I'm afraid of dogs.
_____ 17. She wasn't a good student, but she wound up becoming a successful businesswoman.

a. I almost did, but I got cold feet.
b. No, you're wrong! I'm thinking about getting married.
c. I can't now, but I'll be able to when I'm through.
d. I can't tell.
e. No, don't. I know that deep down you don't really want to. I'll find someone else to do it.
f. I always thought she was smart.
g. I know, but I had second thoughts when I realized how expensive the trip would be.
h. Why don't you stop complaining and get yourself a glass of water?
i. It looks like we have a lot in common.
j. How can he afford those things?
k. Cut it out! I told you not to tell anyone. Can't you keep a secret?
l. Single.
m. You know how it is. History always repeats itself because people don't learn from their mistakes.
n. Do your parents know what you want to do?
o. Sure. Shoot!
p. Hurry up and tell me. I'm dying to hear.
q. No problem. I'll put him outside.

Lesson 1 **Answer Key**

Exercise 1

1. cold feet
2. don't have second thoughts
3. can tell
4. am dying to
5. get married
6. have a lot in common
7. deep down
8. through with

Exercise 2

1. o	2. c	3. j	4. h	5. k	6. a
7. p	8. d	9. b	10. g	11. e	12. l
13. n	14. m	15. i	16. q	17. f	

Guess Who?

誰だと思う？

Lesson 2

D·I·A·L·O·G·U·E

PETER: Guess who?

LAURA: José? No. not José. Peter! I can't believe it! I haven't seen you **in ages**. How are you?

PETER: Pretty good.

LAURA: Can you join me?

PETER: I wish I could, but I'**m on my way** out. I have to be in the city in an hour.

LAURA: **Come on.** Just for a minute.

PETER: There's a lot of traffic and I really have to **get going**. Listen, you know where I live—why don't you **drop in** one evening?

LAURA: I'll do that. And **feel free to drop in on** me, too. Let's **keep in touch**.

PETER: I'd really like to. Talk to you soon. I'm glad I **ran into** you. Take care.

ピーター： 誰だと思う?

ローラ： ホセ? いや、違うわ。ピーター! 信じられないわ! ずいぶん長いこと会ってなかったわね。元気にしてる?

ピーター： 元気だよ。

ローラ： 一緒にどう?

ピーター： そうしたいんだけど、いま出るところなんだ。一時間で町に行かなきゃいけないんだよ。

ローラ： いいじゃない。ちょっとだけ。

ピーター： 道も混んでるし、本当に行かなきゃ。ねえ、僕の住んでる所知ってるでしょ? そのうち晩にでもおいでよ。

ローラ： そうするわ。私の所にも遠慮しないで来てね。連絡とりあいましょう。

ピーター： そうだね。またそのうちね。偶然会えてよかったよ。じゃあね。

➜ 1. **Guess who?**　Can you guess who I am? の省略と考えられる。
7. **in an hour**　時間の経過を表す。Lesson 1の注(5ページ)参照。
10. **you know where I live**　間接疑問文。語順がwhere do I liveとならないのに注意する。
16. **Take care.**　Take care of yourself.の省略で、直訳すれば「お体を大切に」という意味だが、別れ際にサラッと親しい相手に対して用いる。

Guess Who? • 23

17 in/for ages

長い間

- **A:** How's Tony these days?
- **B:** I don't know. I haven't seen him **in/for ages**.

- **A:** We've been in this traffic **for ages**.
- **B:** We sure have. I want to go home.

- **A:** トニーは近頃元気かな。
- **B:** 分からないや。ずっと会ってないから。

- **A:** ずいぶん長いこと車が流れないね。
- **B:** 本当ね。家に帰りたいわ。

➙ 現在完了形の動詞と一緒に用いられる。

18 be on one's way/be on the way

〜へ行くところだ

- **A:** Where are you?
- **B:** I'**m on my way** home.

- **A:** Hi, is Mollie there?
- **B:** Is this Heather? No, she just left. She'**s on her way** to your house.

- **A:** 今どこ？
- **B:** 家に帰るところだ。

- **A:** もしもし、モリーはいますか？
- **B:** ヘザーかしら？いいえ、あの子はちょうど出たわ。あなたの家へ向かっているところよ。

❖ **be out of one's way**　「へんぴな、ずいぶん離れた」

A: I can stop at the store before I pick you up.
B: No, don't. The store **is out of your way** and we don't have time.

A: あなたを乗せる前にお店に寄ろうかしらね。
B: だめだよ。店はずいぶん離れたところにあるし時間がないから。

❖ **be in one's way, be in the way**　「じゃまになって」

A: I can't see the movie. That tall guy's head **is in the way**.
B: Tell him to move his head out of your way.

A: (映画の)画面が見えないよ。あののっぽの男の頭がじゃまだ。
B: 頭をどけてもらうように言えば。

19 Come on.
さあこい、がんばれ、さあ行こう、急げ、よせよ

A: I really can't stay.
B: **Come on.** Stay for five minutes.

A: 本当にもう行かなきゃ。
B: いいじゃない。5分くらいだからさ。

A: I'll never learn English.
B: **Come on.** That's no way to talk.

A: 英語なんて覚えられないや。
B: がんばれよ。そんなこと言うなよ。

A: **Come on.** We're late.

A: 急いで。遅れてるわ。

A: **Come on.** I don't believe you.

A: ばか言うなよ。君の言うことなんて信じないぞ。

➜ 激励・督促・挑発・勧誘などを表す。

Guess Who? • 25

20 get going

出発する

A: The movie starts in twenty minutes. We'd better **get going**.
B: I'll be right there.

A: 映画は20分で始まるよ。**出発**したほうがいい。
B: 今そっちへ行くわ。

➜ start, leave よりもより口語的な表現。

21 drop in/drop by/stop by

立ち寄る、訪れる

A: There's Peter's house. Let's **drop by** and surprise him.
B: I don't think it's a good idea to **drop in** without calling first.
A: I think it's OK to **stop by**.

A: ピーターの家だ。ちょっと**立ち寄って**驚かせてやろうよ。
B: あらかじめ電話もしないで**寄る**なんて良くないと思うな。
A: 僕は(立ち寄っても)いいと思うけどな。

➜ visit よりもより口語的。

❖ **drop in at (a place)/drop in on (a person)「訪れる、訪問する」**

A: Let's **drop in at** Peter's house.
B: That's a good idea. It would be fun to **drop**

A: ピーターの家に**寄って**いこうよ。
B: そりゃいいね。ちょっと彼に**会いに**行くのも楽しいだ

in on him. | ろうね。

➼ call at (a place), call on (a person) よりも少しくだけたひびきがある。

❖ drop off「置いてくる、(車から)降ろす」, pick up「ひろう、受け取る、(車に)乗せる」

A: I have to **drop** my sweater **off** at the cleaners today so I can **pick** it **up** tomorrow.
B: I'll **drop** you **off** at the corner.

A: セーターを今日洗濯屋に**預**けておかなきゃ。そうすれば明日**受け取れる**から。
B: 角のところで**降ろす**よ。

➼ drop offはポトッと何かを落とす感じ、pick upは何かをヒョイとつまみあげる感じ。訳語をただ暗記するよりも、これらの語句が表す具体的な動作を理解すれば文脈に応じた発展的な用法も自然と分かってくる。たとえばpick up a girlは女の子をナンパすることだが、これを語感のレベルでちゃんと理解するためには pick up という語句の表す物理的動作から捉えておく必要がある。

❖ drop out of, drop out「落ちこぼれる、脱落する」, (be a) dropout「落ちこぼれ、脱落者」

A: He **dropped out** of school last year and he still can't find a job.
B: He **dropped out** last year?
A: Yes, it's too bad. I never thought that he'd become a **dropout**.

A: 彼は去年学校を**退学**してまだ仕事が見つからないんだ。
B: 去年**退学**したの?
A: そうだよ。残念だね。彼が**落ちこぼれ**になるなんて考えてもみなかった。

Guess Who? • 27

22 feel free to

遠慮せず〜する

A: It was so nice to see you. I hope we'll be able to get together again soon.
B: Feel free to call me any time.

A: お会いできて嬉しかったです。また近いうちにお会いしたいですね。
B: いつでも**遠慮なく**電話して下さいね。

23 keep/stay in touch (with)/lose touch
連絡をとり続ける／連絡がとだえる

A: It was good talking to you.
B: (Let's) **keep/stay in touch** (with each other).
A: I agree. Let's not **lose touch**.

A: お話できて良かったです。
B: 連絡を取りあいましょうね。
A: そうですね。ご無沙汰ってことにならないように。

❖ **be in touch (with)** 「つき合いがある」

❖ **be out of touch (with)** 「つき合いがとだえている」

A: **Are** you **in touch with** Steve?
B: No, we've **been out of touch** for two years.

A: 最近スティーブとはつき合いがあるの？
B: ううん。この２年くらいご無沙汰なの。

❖ **get back in touch, get in touch again** 「再びつき合いだす、よりが戻る」

A: I thought you two lost touch.
B: We did, but we **got back in touch** when we saw each other at Dorothy's party.

A: 君らふたりはもう縁が切れたかと思った。
B: そうなんだけど、ドロシーのパーティで会ってからまたつき合いが始まったのさ。

Guess Who?

24 run into

偶然に会う

A: I **ran into** our old English teacher in the supermarket. I couldn't believe it.
B: I'll bet you never expected to **run into** her!

A: スーパーで僕らが昔習った英語の先生にばったり会ったよ。信じられない。
B: あの人に出くわすなんて思ってもみなかったろうね。

➤➤ happen to meet, meet by chance よりもくだけた表現。何かにドスンとぶつかっていくような感じ。次の会話は文字どうり「衝突」の意味で用いられている例。

A: Look! That crazy driver **ran into** (= crashed into) a tree.
B: Stop at that phone so we can call an ambulance.

A: ごらん！あの無茶なドライバーが木にぶつかったぞ。
B: あそこの電話のところで止まって救急車を呼ぼう。

e·x·e·r·c·i·s·e·s

1) テープ(CD)を聴いて、次のダイアローグの空欄に適当な語句を書き入れてみましょう。

LIZ: Dick!

DICK: Liz! I never thought I'd (1)_____ you here!
I haven't seen you (2)_____ . How are you?

LIZ: Not bad. How about you?

DICK: Fine. What's new?

LIZ: Nothing special.

DICK: I knew I would see you again sometime, somewhere. Let's pay for our groceries and go get some coffee.

LIZ: Sorry, I can't.

DICK: (3)_____ . You can find five minutes for me.

LIZ: Listen I have to (4)_____ . Please move your shopping cart (5)_____ so I can do my shopping.

DICK: Can I (6)_____ some time so that we can talk? I don't like being (7)_____ with you.

LIZ: I'm really busy.

DICK: Well then, (8)_____ call me any time. You know the number. It was great seeing you.

Guess Who? • 31

e·x·e·r·c·i·s·e·s

2 次の1〜12の文に対する返答として適当なものを33ページのa〜lより選んでみましょう。

_____ 1. Why don't you stay for a while?
_____ 2. I hate to say good-bye, but it's time to board the plane.
_____ 3. Thanks for dropping in.
_____ 4. I can't make a speech in front of the whole class!
_____ 5. Did you see what happened?
_____ 6. Why are you in a hurry?
_____ 7. I have to set the table for dinner, but the table is full of books.
_____ 8. I saw my old girlfriend at the café.
_____ 9. This movie is terrible. It's so long and boring.
_____ 10. Have you seen Margaret lately?
_____ 11. Can you give me a ride home?
_____ 12. I have to stop at the bank.

a. Let me help you move them out of the way.
b. Because I'm late for work.
c. No problem. You're on my way.
d. Let's go. It feels like we've been here for ages.
e. No, I haven't seen her in ages.
f. No, because people were in my way.
g. Do we have to? It's out of our way and we'll be late.
h. Remember to keep in touch.
i. Did you run into her, or did you plan to meet?
j. I wish I could, but I have an appointment so I have to get going.
k. It was great talking to you.
l. Come on. You can do it!

LESSON 2 Answer Key

Exercise 1

1. run into
2. in ages
3. Come on
4. get going
5. out of my way
6. drop in
7. out of touch
8. feel free to

Exercise 2

1. j (*or* b)	2. h	3. k	4. l	5. f	6. b
7. a	8. i	9. d	10. e	11. c	12. g

Please Leave a Message After You Hear the Beep

発信音の後で メッセージをどうぞ

Lesson
3

D·I·A·L·O·G·U·E

TELEPHONE RECORDING: This is 510-2878. **Please leave a message after you hear the beep.**

MELISSA (thinking): Oh, no. I can't do it... Everyone has an answering machine these days. It's really **a pain**. I'm going to **go out of my mind**. I'm going to **hang up** ... but I have to **leave a message**. I know, I'll **write it down** so I can **call back** and read it... Where's a pencil?... OK... I'll say, "Hi, **this is** Melissa. I'm calling about the apartment for rent. Please call me back at 415-2550. I'm usually here in the evening. Thank you." OK... Where's that number?

STEVE: Melissa—What**'s going on**? You look so nervous. Can you **stand still** for a minute?

MELISSA: No, I can't. I'm trying to **get up the**

留守録: こちら 510-2878 です。発信音が聞こえたらメッセージをお願いします。

メリサ: ああ、やだ、こんなのできない...近頃みんな留守番電話なんだから。私これ本当に苦手なのよね。気が変になるわ。切っちゃおうかしら。でもメッセージを入れておかなくちゃ。そうだ、まず紙に書いておいてからまた電話して読んじゃおう。鉛筆はどこだっけ。よーし、これでどうかしら。「もしもし、こちらメリサです。賃貸のアパートの件でお電話しました。415-2550までお電話お願いします。晩は大抵ここにいますので。ではよろしくお願いします。」これでよしと...番号はどこだったっけ?

ステイーブ: メリサ、一体どうしたんだい? すごくひきつってるけど。ちょっと落ち着いていられないの?

メリサ: だめよ。いまなんとか勇気を振り絞って人の留守番電話にメッセージを入れようと思ってるんだから。

D·I·A·L·O·G·U·E

nerve to leave a message on someone's answering machine.

STEVE: You're afraid of answering machines?

MELISSA: Uh-huh. I **freeze** and **get tongue-tied**, and I don't really know why. I just don't like talking into a machine.

STEVE: Want me to do it for you?

MELISSA: Thanks, but I think I should do this **on my own**. I wrote down what I want to say and I **was just about ready to** call and leave a message when you walked in.

STEVE: **Good for you.** Do you want me to leave while you **make your call**?

MELISSA: **Don't be silly.** Just **have a seat** and **wish me luck**! OK now... I'd better **take a deep breath** first... all right... **here goes!**

ステイーブ: 留守番電話が怖いの?

メリサ: うん。金縛りにあって口がきけなくなるのよ。なぜだかよく分からないんだけど。とにかく機械に話しかけるのは苦手なの。

ステイーブ: 代わりにやってあげようか?

メリサ: ありがとう。でも自分でやらなくちゃ。言いたいことを書きつけてちょうどメッセージを入れようとしてたところであなたが入ってきたの。

ステイーブ: そりゃよかった。電話するあいだここから出て行こうか?

メリサ: バカ言わないで。座って私のために祈っててちょうだい。さてと、これでよし...まず深呼吸しなくちゃ...よーし、いくわよ!

➤➤ **17. You look so nervous.** look + 形容詞で「〜に見える」の意味。

23. be afraid of + 名詞／動名詞で「〜(すること)がこわい」。

24. Uh-huh 相手の質問に対して肯定で答えるときに用いる、非常にくだけた表現。

27. Want me to do it for you? Do you want me to do it for you? が省略されたもの。want A to do で「Aに〜してもらいたい」の意味。

Please Leave a Message After You Hear the Beep • 39

25 Please leave a message after (you hear) the beep.

発信音の後でメッセージを残して下さい

A: You have reached 209-1764. No one can come to the phone right now. **Please leave a message after the beep** and we'll call you back. (*beep*)

B: Hi Russ. Want to have lunch at 12? Leave a message on my machine to let me know. I'll be **checking my messages**.

A: あなたは 209-1764 におかけになりましたが、ただいま留守にしております。**発信音の後でメッセージをお願いします。**こちらから折り返しご連絡致します。(ピーッ)

B: もしもし、ラス？ 12時にお昼でも一緒にどう？ 私の留守電に返事を入れておいてね。ときどきメッセージをチェックしてるから。

26 a pain

やっかいなもの／人

A: Writing letters is **a pain** for me. I'd rather call someone.

B: I'm exactly the opposite. I'd much rather write than call.

A: 手紙を書くのって**苦手**なの。電話のほうがいいわ。

B: 私は正反対のタイプね。電話するより手紙のほうがずっといいの。

❖ a pain in the neck 「やっかいなもの／人」

- Leaving messages on answering machines is **a pain in the neck** for me.
- Writing letters is **a pain in the neck** for me.
- They are really **a pain in the neck**. They always want something from us.

― 私、留守番電話にメッセージ入れるのってどうもだめなのよね。

― 手紙を書くのって何だかしんどくって。

― あの人達って本当に**勘弁**してよってかんじ。いつも私たちを利用しようとするんですもの。

27 go out of one's mind

気が狂う

A: I have so much to do that I'm **going out of my mind**.
B: Maybe you need to take a break.

A: やることがありすぎて**気が変になりそうだ**。
B: ちょっと休んだほうがいいんじゃないか。

❖ **be out of one's mind** 「気が狂っている」

A: You'**re out of your mind**! Why are you driving so fast in this traffic?
B: They **are out of their minds**. How can they ride their bikes at night without lights?

A: **気でもふれたんじゃないの**？ こんな所でそんなに飛ばすなんて。
B: **おかしいのはあいつらだ**よ。ライトもつけないで夜バイクを乗り回すなんてどういうつもりなんだ。

➻ 類似表現としてはbe/go nuts, be/go bananas, be/go off one's rockerなどがあるが、be/go out of one's mindよりもずっとくだけた表現。

28 hang up

(電話を)切る

A: I'm sorry. I need to **hang up** right now because someone's at my door.
B: OK. I'll talk to you at

A: ごめんなさい。もう**切ら**なくちゃ。玄関に誰か来てるの。
B: あっそう。じゃ学校でね。

42 • Lesson 3

school.

❖ **hang up on (*someone*)** 「(怒っていきなり電話を)切る」

A: I don't believe you at all!
B: That's O.K. with me! (B **hangs up on** A without saying good-bye.)

A: おまえの言うことなんて信じられるかよ！
B: いいわよ！（怒ってさよならも言わずにいきなり電話を切る）

29 write *something* down
(紙などに)書きつける

A: My phone number is 642-5933. Can you remember that?
B: Probably not. I'd better **write** it **down**. Do you have a pen?

A: 私の電話番号は642-5933よ。覚えられる？
B: たぶん無理ね。書いといたほうがいいみたい。ペンか何かある？

➤➤ put something down も同じ意味で用いられる。

Please Leave a Message After You Hear the Beep • 43

30 be going on

起こっている

A: What's **going on** in here? Who are all these people?
B: Oh, hi, Dad. We're having a party. I hope it's OK . . .

A: What's new?
B: Oh, **there's** so much **going on**. My sister just had a baby, our dog ran away, we're going to move . . .

A: いったいどういうことだ(ここで何が**起きている**のか)。この連中は何なんだ。
B: ああ、お父さん。パーティだよ。ねっ、いいよね?

A: 何か変わったことある?
B: もう**大変なもんよ**(とても多くのことが**起きている**)。お姉さんには赤ちゃんが生まれるし、私たちの犬はいなくなっちゃうし、それに私たち引っ越すの。

➺ be happeningと同じ意味。進行形で用いられるのが普通。

31 stand still

じっとしている

A: Uh-oh—you'd better **stand still**. There's a bee on your shirt.
B: Oh no! Get it off!

A: Listen, I'll fix your hair if you'll just **stand still**.

A: おっとっと、**動かない**ほうがいいよ。シャツに蜂がとまってる。
B: やーだ! 追っ払って!

A: あのね、髪直してあげるから**じっとしてて**。

B: I am **standing still**.
A: No, you aren't. You keep moving and I can't do this.

B: (じっと)してるわよ。
A: だめ、動いてるから出来ないじゃない。

32 get up the nerve (to do ...)
勇気を出して〜する

A: I want to ask her to marry me, but **I can't get up the nerve to ask**.
B: Are you afraid that she'll say no?

A: 彼女に結婚を申し込みたいんだけど、**なかなか言い出せなくって**。
B: ノーと言われるのがこわいの？

A: I've been working there for two years without a raise, and I need to **get up the nerve to** talk to my boss.
B: You really should. Do you want to practice on me?

A: あそこで2年間ずっと働いてきて昇給がないんだもんな。思いきって上司に話さなきゃいけないよね。
B: 本当だね。まず僕を相手に予行演習でもしてみるかい？

➸ get the courage to do something よりもくだけた表現。また、have the nerve to do something だと「厚かましくも〜する」となる。*cf. He had the nerve to break into the line.* (厚かましくも列に割り込んだ)

Please Leave a Message After You Hear the Beep • 45

33 freeze

(恐怖や緊張で)動けなくなる

A: When I got to the front of the class to make my speech, I **froze** and forgot everything I was going to say.
B: Then what happened?
A: My teacher reminded me to use my notes.

A: クラスのみんなの前でスピーチをしようとしたら**コチコチになって**言うこと忘れちゃった。
B: それでどうしたの？
A: 先生にメモを使うよう言われたんだ。

➥ 本来の意味は「凍りつく」であることから、まるで凍ったように動けないという意味に用いられるようになった。銃を突きつけて Freeze! と言えば「動くな！」となる。

34 get tongue-tied

(あがって)話せなくなる

A: I always **get tongue-tied** when I talk to people who have power.
B: What do you mean?
A: Oh, you know, people like teachers and bosses. They make me so nervous that I can't talk.

A: エライ人と話すときいつも**舌がまわらなくなる**んだ。
B: どういうこと？
A: ほら、学校の先生とか上司とか。緊張してちゃんと話せなくなるんだ。

❖ be tongue-tied 「(あがって)話ができない」

A: Come on. Tell me what happened.
B: Uh... I...
A: What happened? **Are** you **tongue-tied** all of a sudden?

A: おい、いったいどうしたのか言ってごらん。
B: あのー、私...
A: どうしたんだ? 急に**口がきけなくなった**のか?

35 do *something* on one's own
自分でする

A: Mom, I need help with my math homework. I don't understand this.
B: You're already 22 years old! You should be able to **do** your homework **on your own** by now.

A: お母さん、宿題手伝って。これわかんない。
B: あんたもう22でしょ! もう宿題ぐらい**自分で**できなきゃ。

A: Let me help you.
B: No, thanks. I'd rather **do** it **on my own**.

A: お手伝いしましょう。
B: いいえ、結構。**自分で**やりますから。

❖ do *something* (by) *oneself* 「自分でする」

A: Let me help you.
B: No, thanks. I'd rather **do** it **(by) myself**.

A: お手伝いしましょう。
B: いいえ、結構。**自分で**やりますから。

A: Why don't you help him?
B: I offered to help, but he said he wanted to **do** it **by himself**.

A: 彼を手伝ってあげれば?
B: そう言ったんだけど**自分で**やりたいってさ。

Please Leave a Message After You Hear the Beep

36 be (just) about (ready) to do ...
ちょうど〜しようとしているところだ

A: Hello?
B: Irene? Hi! This is Nicole. You sound like you're in a hurry.
A: I'm sorry. I am. **I was just about (ready) to** leave. Can I call you back tonight?
B: Sure. I'll be home around seven.

A: もしもし?
B: アイリーン? やあ、ニコルだよ。急いでるみたいだね。
A: ごめんなさい、そうなの。ちょうど出かけるところだったの。今晩私から電話してもいいかしら?
B: うん。7時ぐらいには家にいるよ。

37 Good for you!
それはよかった

A: I'm going to get a job working with disabled children.
B: **Good for you!**

A: 障害児のための仕事をすることにしたの。
B: そりゃいいね!

A: I got an A on my test!/ I got the job!/ I finished my homework.
B: **Good for you!**

A: テストでA取ったよ!／仕事みつかった!／宿題終わった!
B: よかったね!

➺ 相手が何か良いことをしようとしているとき、または既にしたときに用いる表現。That's great. とも言う。

48 • Lesson 3

38 Don't be silly!

バカなこと言うな(するな)よ

- **A:** Come on. I'll be glad to drive you home.
- **B:** But it's so far.
- **A: Don't be silly!** It's not that far. Let's go.

- **A:** さあ、家まで車で送るよ。
- **B:** だけど遠いし。
- **A:** 何言ってんだよ、そんなでもないじゃない。じゃ行こうか。

➼ Don't be ridiculous! とほぼ同じ。

39 Have a seat.

かけて下さい

- **A:** Come on in and **have a seat**. I'll be right with you.
- **B:** Thanks.

- **A:** さあこちらにいらしておかけになって。すぐ戻りますから。
- **B:** どうも。

➼ sit down よりもていねいで親しみがこもった表現。

Please Leave a Message After You Hear the Beep • 49

40 Wish me luck!

幸運を祈ってね

A: You'd better get going now. Your interview is in an hour, isn't it?
B: Yeah, you're right. **Wish me luck!**
A: Good luck. Don't worry. You'll get the job. Just be yourself.

A: もう出かけたほうがいいよ。面接まであと一時間だろ。
B: ええ、そうね。**幸運を祈っててね。**
A: うん。心配するなって。うまくいくさ。普段のままでいけよ。

➜ 何か新しいことを始めようとするときに用いる表現。

41 take a deep breath

深呼吸する

A: You're next. **Take a deep breath**, and then go to the front of the class.
B: I'm really nervous.

A: 次だよ。**深呼吸**したらクラスのみんなの前に行くんだ。
B: 本当に緊張するな。

(Doctor:) **Take a deep breath** and then breathe out slowly.

(医師：) ゆっくり息を吸って、そしたら今度はゆっくりはいて。

➜ be out of breath なら「息が切れて」、have bad breath は「息が臭い」となる。

42 Here goes!

行くぞ！

A: Do you really expect me to jump out of this airplane?
B: Sure. You've got your parachute on and we've talked all about it. Well?
A: You're right. OK. **Here goes!** (Ahhhhhhhhhh!)

A: This water is so cold!
B: No, it isn't. Just jump in and you'll be OK.
A: All right. You'd better be right. **Here goes!** ... God! It's freezing!

A: 本当にこの飛行機から飛びおりろって言うんですか？
B: そうですよ。ちゃんとパラシュートもつけてるし、ぜんぶ説明もしましたよね。さあ、いいでしょ？
A: そうですね。よし、**行くぞ**！(ウワーッ！)

A: この水冷たい！
B: そうでもないさ。飛び込んでごらん、大丈夫だから。
A: うん、そうだよね。**ヨッシャ**！...うわー、冷たいのなんのって！

➼ 何かちょっと怖いことを始める直前に用いる表現。

Please Leave a Message After You Hear the Beep

e·x·e·r·c·i·s·e·s

1. テープ(CD)を聴いて、次のダイアローグの空欄に適当な語句を書き入れてみましょう。

TELEPHONE RECORDING: Thank you for calling. If you have a touch-tone phone and would like information about your phone bill, press 1 now. If you would like to change your service or arrange new telephone service, press 2 now. If you would like information about our telephone store, press 3 now. If you have a rotary phone, please stay on the line and an operator will help you shortly.

MELISSA: I (1) _____ ! Every time I pick up a phone, I hear a machine. I guess I should press 2... Boy, they really play terrible music while they make you wait.

(*5 minutes later*)

MELISSA: What's (2) _____ here? I've been waiting at least five minutes. I'll have to (3) _____ later ... Hello? Oh, I (4) _____ to (5) _____ .

OPERATOR: Sorry to keep you waiting. How may I help you?

MELISSA: Hi. I'd like to cancel my "call waiting" service.

OPERATOR: May I have your number please?

52 • Lesson 3

MELISSA: 415-2550.

OPERATOR: OK. We can put that change into effect starting tomorrow morning. May I ask your reason for canceling this service?

MELISSA: Sure. My friends don't like the interruption. They say they would rather hear
(6)_____ than hear me say,
" (7)_____ .
(8)_____?" To be honest with you, I don't like the interruption either.

・・
➻ a touch-tone phone 日本語で「プッシュホン」のこと。
a rotary phone 日本語では「ダイアル式電話」のこと。
"call waiting service" 日本の「キャッチホン」のこと。

Please Leave a Message After You Hear the Beep • 53

e·x·e·r·c·i·s·e·s

次の**1〜14**の文に対する返答として適当なものを55ページの**a〜n**より選んでみましょう。

_____ 1. Have a seat. I'll be right with you.
_____ 2. I'm going to write an article for the school newspaper about the educational system in my native country.
_____ 3. What's going on in here? Why are the lights out?
_____ 4. Oh, I have another call. Can you hold on for a minute?
_____ 5. The homework for tomorrow is on pages 36, 42, 45, 46, 49, and 50.
_____ 6. Please leave a message after you hear the beep.
_____ 7. Didn't you call Larry?
_____ 8. This traffic is a real pain in the neck. I'm going to get a job closer to home.
_____ 9. If you don't stand still, I won't be able to take your picture.
_____ 10. I was just about to go to bed when the phone rang and I got the news.
_____ 11. Your whole family can stay in my house.
_____ 12. Let me help you.
_____ 13. How did you get up the nerve to say that?
_____ 14. When the teacher asked her why she copied her friend's homework, she was tongue-tied.

a. I'd better write that down.
b. Do you think you can find one?
c. Hi, Joni? This is Jean. Can you call me back? Thanks.
d. Thanks, but I should try to do it on my own.
e. Thanks.
f. I did, but his line was busy.
g. She must have been really embarrassed.
h. Then you should use your video camera instead.
i. Good for you!
j. I bet you had trouble falling asleep.
k. Surprise! Happy Birthday!
l. Don't be silly! You don't have enough room.
m. Well. first I took a deep breath, and then I looked him in the eye and told him.
n. Only for a minute. I'm in a hurry.

Lesson 3 Answer Key

Exercise 1
1. am going out of my mind
2. going on
3. call back
4. was just about ready
5. hang up
6. a busy signal
7. Sorry, I have another call.
8. Can you hold on

Exercise 2

1. e	2. i	3. k	4. n	5. a	6. c
7. f	8. b	9. h	10. j	11. l	12. d
13. m	14. g				

In Bad Shape

調子が悪い

Lesson 4

D·I·A·L·O·G·U·E

CARMEN: Hello?

NICK: Carmen? Is that you? Are you OK?

CARMEN: Uh-uh, I **caught a** terrible **cold**.

NICK: You too? Well, **I have news for you. We're in the same boat**! Ahchoo!

CARMEN: Bless you.

NICK: Thanks.

CARMEN: Why don't you come over and **keep me company**? I haven't talked to anyone **all day long**.

NICK: I'd like to, but I **can't stop** sneez**ing**. Ahchoo! Ahchoo! And I have a sore throat. I just want to go to bed.

CARMEN: **I know what you mean.** Do you have a fever?

NICK: I don't know for sure, but I think so. I was going to **take my temperature**, but I dropped the thermometer and it broke.

CARMEN: **It sounds like** you should just...

カルメン: もしもし?

ニック: カルメン? 君かい? だいじょうぶ?

カルメン: うーん、ひどいカゼなの。

ニック: 君も? 実を言うとね、僕もカゼなんだ。ハクション!

カルメン: あらお大事に。

ニック: こりゃどうも。

カルメン: こっちへ来て私の相手になってよ。一日中誰も話す人がないの。

ニック: そうしたいけど、くしゃみが止まらないんだ。ハクション! ハクション! それにのども痛いし、寝ていたいよ。

カルメン: わかるわ。熱はあるの?

ニック: どうかなあ。もしかしてあるかもしれない。熱を測ろうと思っていたら体温計を落として割っちゃったんだ。

カルメン: どうやらあなたは...ハックション! ごめんなさい。あなたはアスピリンでものんで寝たほうがいいみたいね。そうすればたぶん朝には気分が良くなるんじゃないかな。

D·I·A·L·O·G·U·E

ahchoo! Excuse me. You should just take two aspirin and go to bed. **Chances are** you'll feel better in the morning.

NICK: I hope so. And I hope you'll **get over** your cold soon. Are you going to school tomorrow?

CARMEN: I don't think so. I**'m in** really **bad shape**. I may have to be absent for a few more days.

NICK: Listen to us! We **feel sorry for** ourselves today, don't we?

ニック： そうだといいけど。早くこのカゼをのりきらなくちゃ。明日は学校へ行くの?

カルメン： 無理だと思うわ。本当に調子が悪いの。私あと何日か休むかもしれない。

ニック： あーあ! 今日はふたりで落ち込んじゃったね。

➨ **2. Is that you?**　電話では自分や相手をthis/thatで指す。
cf. Hello, this is Bob. Is that you, Cathy?
6. Bless you.　元来は「神の祝福あれ」の意味だが、くしゃみをした人に言う決まり文句。くしゃみは不吉の前兆とされるため、縁起をかついでこのような言いまわしを用いる。

43 catch/have a cold
カゼをひく／ひいている

A: You'd better not come near me. I have a terrible sore throat. and I can't stop sneezing.

B: You **caught** another **cold**? I hope you don't **have the flu**.

A: 近くに来ないほうがいいよ。のどがすごく痛くって、くしゃみが止まらないんだよ。

B: また**カゼをひいた**のかい？**流感**でなければいいけど。

44 I have/I've got news for you.
あなたに言うことがあります

A: He just told me that I won't be able to work here any more.

B: **I have news for you.** He just told the same thing to twenty other people.

A: 僕はもうここで働けないって言われちゃったよ。

B: **いいこと教えてあげようか**。あの人同じこと他に20人ぐらいの人に言ってるんだよ。

➻ 聞き手にとって未知の事がらを言い出す前に用いる表現。

45 be in the same boat

同じ運命にある

A: I'll have to stay up all night to study for that exam.
B: I**'m in the same boat**! I'll have to stay up, too.
A: Why don't we study together?

A: I can't believe that we got a flat tire.
B: Look across the street. Those people **are in the same boat**!

A: 例のテスト準備で徹夜しなくちゃいけないんだ。
B: 僕もそうなんだ。徹夜だよ。
A: 一緒に勉強しようか？

A: パンクなんて信じられない！
B: 道の向こう側をごらん。あの人たちも**同じめにあって**るよ。

➼ 「同じ船に乗っている」が文字通りの意味で、ここから転じて「同じ状況にある」の意味で、通常あまり好ましくない事がらに用いられる。

In Bad Shape

46 keep *someone* company

相手をする

A: I have to go now.
B: Please don't go yet. **Keep me company** for just a little while.

A: Are you going alone? Do you want someone to **keep you company**?
B: Sure! That would be great!

A: もう行かなきゃ。
B: まだ行かないで。もう少しだけつき合って。

A: ひとりで行くの？誰かについて行ってほしい？
B: ええ！そうしてもらえると本当に嬉しいわ！

➻ keep company with A は「A（しばしば異性）と交際する」、part company with A なら「Aと絶交する、別れる」となる。これらは be going out with A「Aとつき合う」、break up with A「Aと別れる」よりもあらたまった感じがする。

47 all day (long)/all night (long)

一日中／一晩中

A: My eyes hurt.
B: I'm not surprised. You've been reading that book **all day long**.

A: 目が痛い。
B: そりゃそうだろ。その本一日中読んでたんだから。

48 can't stop —ing
〜するのをやめられない

A: What am I going to do? I **can't stop smoking**.
B: If you really wanted to, you would.

A: どうしよう、タバコやめられないよ。
B: 本気になれば出来るはずだよ。

❖ **can't stop to** *do* 「〜するため(いましていることを)やめられない」

A: Can you stop writing for a while? I want to discuss something with you.
B: I **can't stop to talk** now. I have to finish this report.

A: ちょっと書きものするのやめてくれない？ 話があるの。
B: 今ちょっと手が離せない。この報告書を仕上げなくちゃいけないんだ。

49 I know what you mean.
あなたの言いたいこと、分かります

A: He's always telling people what to do.
B: **I know what you mean.** My uncle is like that.

A: 彼はいつも人に指図ばっかりしてるんだ。
B: わかるよ。僕のおじさんもそうだから。

❖ **What do you mean?** 「どういうことですか」

A: He's very bossy.
B: **What do you mean?**
A: Well, he's always telling people what to do.

A: 彼はとってもエバッてるよ。
B: どういうこと？
A: うん、いつも他人に指図ばっかするんだ。

In Bad Shape • 65

50 take *someone's* temperature

体温をはかる

- **A:** Her forehead seems warm.
- **B:** Let's get the thermometer and **take her temperature**.

- **A:** 彼女のおでこ熱いみたいだ。
- **B:** 体温計を取ってきて**熱をはかって**みよう。

❖ **have a fever, have fever** 「熱がある」

- **A:** Her temperature is 101°F (38.3°C).
- **B:** Well, normal is only 98.6°F (37°C). She **has a fever**.
- **A:** Let's call the doctor.

- **A:** 彼女の体温は101度(摂氏38.3度)ある。
- **B:** うーん。平熱は98.6度(摂氏37度)だから**熱がある**ね。
- **A:** お医者さんを呼ぼう。

51 sound(s) like (+ *noun phrase*)
sound(s) + *adjective*

〜のようだ

- **A:** I have three exams next week.

- **A:** 来週3つも試験があるんだ。

66 • Lesson 4

B: It **sounds like** school is keeping you busy.

B: 学校のことで忙しいみたいだね。

A: Have you seen any reviews of that new movie?
B: Yes, I've seen a few. It **sounds** great.

A: あの新しい映画の批評みた?
B: うん、まあね。素晴らしいみたいだね。

➨ It seems that (*or* as if) … よりも口語的。
➨ It seems (to be) … よりも口語的。

❖ sound (文字通りの意味で)「音がする」

A: Have you heard Mike play his violin?
B: Yes, I have. He **sounds** awful.
A: Well, he's had only one lesson.

A: マイクがバイオリン弾くの聞いた?
B: ええ、本当にひどい音ね。
A: まあ、まだ一回しかレッスンしてないんだから。

52 chances are
おそらく、たぶん

A: Where's Gary?
B: He was sneezing a lot last night. **Chances are** he's staying home today.

A: ゲーリーはどこ?
B: きのうの晩ずいぶんくしゃみしてた。たぶん今日は家にいるんじゃないかな。

➨ maybe, probably などの副詞と同様の働きをする。It is likely that … よりも口語的な表現。

In Bad Shape • 67

53 get over *something/someone*

回復する

A: I have an important appointment next week. I'd **better get over** this cold by then.
B: Well, don't go back to work until you're feeling better.

A: 来週は大事な約束があるの。それまでにこのカゼ何とかしなくちゃ。
B: そう、気分が良くなるまでまだ仕事したらだめだよ。

A: Carol's boyfriend left her two months ago, and she still hasn't **gotten over** him.
B: Let's introduce her to Jerry. She might like him.

A: キャロルは2ヵ月前に彼氏にふられてまだ**立ち直って**ないの。
B: ジェリーに紹介してあげよう。気にいるかもしれないよ。

➦ 壁などの障害物を「乗り越える」が本来の意味。ここから転じて病気を克服したり、失恋から立ち直るといった場合にも用いられる。

54. be in good/bad shape
調子がいい／調子が悪い

A: How are you doing?
B: I'**m in bad shape**. I have a sore throat and a high fever.

A: 元気？
B: 調子悪いよ。のどは痛いし熱はずいぶんあるし。

A: You look like you'**re in** really **good shape.**
B: Thanks. I've been exercising.

A: 本当に元気そうだね。
B: ありがとう。運動続けてるから。

➻ 体調だけではなく、精神的な状態にも用いられる。

A: How are you doing?
B: I'**m in** pretty **good shape**. No big problems. And you?

A: 元気？
B: もう絶好調。困ったこともないし。君は？

A: How are you doing?
B: I'**m in bad shape**. I have two books to read for school and I haven't even started them.

A: 調子どう？
B: もうダメ。学校で読まなきゃいけない本が2冊もあるのにまだ始めてもいないんだ。

55 feel sorry for (*someone*)

気の毒に思う

A: Why did you give that guy a dollar?
B: I **feel sorry for** him.

A: Look at him. His girlfriend left him and now he **feels sorry for** himself.
B: He'll get over her soon.

A: なんであんなやつに1ドルあげたの？
B: 気の毒だったから。

A: 彼をごらん。彼女にふられて落ち込んでるんだ。
B: じきに忘れられるよ。

➜ 相手に直接 I feel sorry for you. と言うのは失礼になる。また、I'm sorry. は相手に不幸があったときなどにも慰めの意味で用いることがあるので注意を要する。

e·x·e·r·c·i·s·e·s

> テープ(CD)を聴いて、次のダイアローグの空欄に適当な語句を書き入れてみましょう。

VET: So, what seems to be the problem?
MAN: Tuck was awake (1)_____ .
And this morning he wouldn't eat anything. And look, he (2)_____ pulling on his right ear.
VET: It (3)_____ something is wrong. Will you help me hold him so I can (4)_____ ? Thanks... Yes, he does have a fever.
MAN: I (5)_____ him. Look at his sad eyes.
VET: (6)_____ he'll be better by tomorrow. These pills will help him (7)_____ his infection quickly.
MAN: What infection?
VET: He has an ear infection.
MAN: Really? We (8)_____ . I have an ear infection too!
VET: That is a coincidence. But you look like you (9)_____ .
MAN: I'm better now because I've been taking medicine.
VET: And that's exactly what Tuck will do. You can pick him up tomorrow.
MAN: (10)_____ ?

In Bad Shape • 71

e·x·e·r·c·i·s·e·s

VET: I mean that I'd like to keep him here overnight.
MAN: But I live alone! I need him to (11)_____ .
VET: It's only for one night.
MAN: (12)_____ . One night is a long time. Tuck is coming home with me!

2 次の1～16の文に対する返答として適当なものを73ページのa～qより選んでみましょう。

_____ 1. Bless you!
_____ 2. Amy! I haven't seen you in a long time! Have you been sick?
_____ 3. I'd better hurry so I can catch the 11 o'clock bus.
_____ 4. I missed my flight and can't get another one 'til 2 a.m.
_____ 5. You were in a car accident, weren't you?
_____ 6. Ron is staying with you? That's nice.
_____ 7. Did you have a good time?
_____ 8. Do you like the dinner?
_____ 9. Let's take a break and have lunch. You've been working all morning.
_____ 10. It's hard to say the English "th" sound because you have to put your tongue between your teeth.
_____ 11. He has a high fever.
_____ 12. Do you know when she'll be home?
_____ 13. They had dinner out, and then they went to a

movie.

_____ **14.** What a movie! People were killing each other for two hours.

_____ **15.** Do you want to go to the zoo?

_____ **16.** Forget about Jeff. There are lots of other men in the world.

a. I know, but I can't stop to eat until I finish what I'm doing.
b. I know, but I'll never get over him.
c. Mmm. It's delicious. I can't stop eating.
d. It sounds like they had a good time.
e. I know what you mean. I have the same problem.
f. Thanks. I guess I caught a cold.
g. Yes, he's keeping me company while my room mate is away.
h. Uh-huh. I had the flu, but I'm OK now.
i. Uh-huh. But don't worry. I'm in good shape now.
j. It was great. We laughed all night long.
k. No I don't. I got over it.
l. I have news for you. It's already 11:30.
m. Maybe he should go to the doctor.
n. You know, I'm in the same boat. Why don't we go into the city for a few hours?
o. She said around 9, so chances are she'll be here soon.
p. It sounds terrible.
q. Not really. I always feel so sorry for those poor animals in cages.

Lesson 4 Answer Key

Exercise 1
1. all night long
2. can't stop
3. sounds like
4. take his temperature
5. feel sorry for
6. Chances are
7. get over
8. are in the same boat
9. are in good shape
10. What do you mean
11. keep me company
12. I have news for you

Exercise 2

1. f	2. h	3. l	4. n	5. i	6. g
7. j	8. c	9. a	10. e	11. m	12. o
13. d	14. p	15. q	16. b		

Are We Couch Potatoes?

僕たちって
カウチ・ポテト族?

Lesson

5

D·I·A·L·O·G·U·E

ANDY: Hi guys. Come on in. You didn't have to bring anything.

SUSAN: We know that, but we wanted to. I'm so glad we could finally **get together**.

RUTH: Let me take your coats. Come in and **make yourselves comfortable**. How are you doing tonight?

MICHAEL: Pretty good. We rented two old movies. What **are you in the mood to** see first —the **tearjerker** or the horror movie?

RUTH: **How about** the horror movie first? I don't **feel like crying** right now. I'd rather **be scared out of my wits**, if I have a choice.

MICHAEL: **That makes two of us**.

アンデイ: やあ、みんな。さあどうぞ。何も持ってこなくてよかったのに。

スーザン: そう言われるとは思ったけど、ちょっとね。やっとみんなで集まれて本当に嬉しいわ。

ルース: コートをどうぞ。お上がりになってくつろいでちょうだい。今晩は調子どう?

マイケル: バッチリさ。古い映画をふたつ借りてきたんだけど、どっちの方から見てみたい? お涙ちょうだいってやつとホラー物とあるけど。

ルース: まずはホラーでどうかしら? 今は泣いてみたい気分じゃないわ。選べるものなら死ぬほど怖がってみたいの。

マイケル: 僕も同じ気分だ。

Are We Couch Potatoes? • 77

D·I·A·L·O·G·U·E

(*During the movie*)

ANDY: Maybe we should turn a light on. This movie is getting a little scary.

RUTH: Andy!

ANDY: **I was just kidding**. Could you **move over** a little? It's getting kind of crowded here.

SUSAN: I'll sit on the floor.

ANDY: No …

SUSAN: Really… I want to. Could you pass the popcorn please?

MICHAEL: **Here you go**. Who has the remote control? Can you **hit pause**? Thanks… I have a question… Do you think we're **couch potatoes**?

ANDY: **Why do you ask?**

MICHAEL: Well, we do **spend a lot of time** sitting on the couch, **glued to the tube** and eating snacks. Sometimes I think I've become **a couch potato**.

(映画の最中に)

アンデイ: ちょっと明かりをつけたほうがいいかな。この映画だんだん怖くなってきたぞ。

ルース: アンデイったら!

アンデイ: 冗談だよ。ちょっとつめてくれるかい? 少し窮屈になってきたから。

スーザン: 床に座るわ。

アンデイ: それはちょっと...

スーザン: いいの。そうしたいの。ポップコーンとってくださる?

マイケル: ホイッと。リモコン誰が持ってるの? ポーズ押してよ。ありがとう...ねえ、聞きたいことがあるんだけど...僕らってカウチ・ポテト族なのかな?

アンデイ: どうしてそんなこときくの?

マイケル: あのね、僕らずいぶん長いことソファーでさあ、テレビにはりついてお菓子食べたりするじゃないか。だから時々自分もカウチ・ポテト族ってやつになっちゃったかなって。

スーザン: 変なの、マイケルったら。あなた本いっぱい読

D·I·A·L·O·G·U·E

SUSAN: **That's funny**, Michael. I thought you **were a bookworm** because you read so much. It's hard to get you to **put a book down**.

MICHAEL: I think I'm watching TV more and reading less...

ANDY: Can we talk about this later? I**'m** really **involved in** this movie. Ruth, will you **hit play**, and Susan, can you pass the popcorn over here please?

むから本の虫かと思ってたのに。あなたに読むの止めさせるの大変ですもの。

マイケル: だんだんテレビを見るのが長く本を読むのが少なくなってきてるような…

アンデイ: こういうことは後で話さない?この映画にすっかりハマッてるんだから。ルース、再生ボタン押して。それとスーザン、ポップコーンこっちに回してくれる?

➡ **3. We know that.** 相手の発言内容をさす。

16. turn a light on 「(電気などを)消す」、反対語は turn off 。

20. It's getting kind of crowded here. kind of は「いくぶん、ある程度」の意味。sort of も同じように用いられる。

Are We Couch Potatoes? • 81

56 get together

□□ **会う、集まる**

A: Do you want to **get together** this weekend?
B: I'd really like to, but let me check my calendar first. I'll call you back.

A: この週末**会お**うか？
B: そうしたいけど、まずカレンダーを見てみないと。また電話するわ。

➽ 食事や遊びなど、社交的な目的で他人と会うこと。なお、次にあげる用例は一緒に用いられる前置詞や接続詞に注意する。

– Let's **get together with** them sometime soon. – 近いうちに**会お**う。
– Let's **get together and** have lunch. – **会って**お昼をご一緒に。
– Let's **get together for** lunch. – **会って**お昼をご一緒に。

57 make oneself comfortable

□□ **楽にする、くつろぐ**

A: Sit down and **make yourself comfortable**. Can I get you a drink?
B: Thanks. I'd love one.

A: お掛けになって**楽にして**下さい。何か飲み物でもお持ちしましょうか？
B: どうも。お願いします。

❖ **make oneself at home**「楽にする、くつろぐ」

A: Come on in and **make yourselves at home**. You can put your coats

A: 上がって**くつろいで**下さい。コートはあそこのベッドの上にどうぞ。

in there on the bed.
B: OK. Thanks.

B: はい、どうもすみません。

➸ 再帰代名詞の変化に注意。I/myself, you/yourself, he/himself, she/herself, we/ourselves, you/yourselves(複数), they/themselves となる。

58 be in the mood to + *verb*/ be in the mood for + *noun*
〜したい／〜が欲しい

A: What do you want to do now?
B: I**'m in the mood to** eat a hamburger.
or I**'m in the mood for** a hamburger.

A: 今何したい？
B: ハンバーガーでも食べたい。

➸ want to do something, want something よりも口語的。be in a good mood「機嫌がいい」, be in a bad mood「機嫌が悪い」。

A: Do you want Chinese or Japanese food tonight?
B: Whatever you want.
A: You**'re in a good mood** today. Did something special happen?

A: 今夜は中華がいい？それとも日本食？
B: 何でもあなたがいいほう。
A: 今日は**機嫌**がいいね。何かいいことあったかな？

A: Don't go near the boss today.
B: Why not?
A: He**'s in a** very **bad mood**.

A: ボスに近寄っちゃだめだよ。
B: どうして？
A: ひどくご**機嫌**ななめなんだ。

59 a tearjerker
悲しい映画

A: Do you have a tissue?
B: I think so. Yeah—here's a clean one. This movie sure is **a tearjerker**.

A: ティッシュある？
B: あると思う。ああ、はい、きれいなやつ。この映画本当に泣けるね。

➡ 「涙をしぼり出すもの」というのが文字通りの意味。

60 How about ... ?
〜はどう？

A: I don't know what to order.
B: **How about** the fish? The salads look good, too.

A: 何を注文したらいいかわかんない。
B: 魚料理**なんかどう？** サラダもおいしそうだね。

A: Who should we invite over for dinner?
B: **How about** Joan and Daniel?

A: 誰を夕食に招待しようか?
B: ジョーンとダニエル**なんかどうかな**?

➼ aboutの後に動詞を用いるときは —ingの形にする。

61 feel like *doing something*
〜したい気分

A: What do you **feel like doing**?
B: I **feel like going** to a movie.

A: 何をしてみたい?
B: 映画にでも行きたい気分ね。

or

A: Why didn't you cook tonight?
B: I **felt like** ordering a pizza instead.

A: 何で今晩はご飯作らなかったの?
B: それよりピザでも注文したかったのよね。

➼ feelを文字通りの意味で用いたのが次の会話。

A: How do you **feel**?
B: Fine/Happy/Tired.

A: 気分はどう?
B: いいです／楽しい／疲れた。

Are We Couch Potatoes? • 85

62 be scared out of one's wits/to death
死ぬほど怖い思いをする

A: How was the movie?
B: Don't see it. I **was scared out of my wits**. I had my eyes closed for almost the whole time.

A: 映画どうだった?
B: 見ちゃだめよ。怖くて死にそうだったわ。ほとんどずっと目をつぶっていたんだから。

❖ **scare** *someone* **out of his/her wits**「誰かを死ぬほど怖がらせる」

A: Aaah! Who's that?
B: It's only me.
A: God! You **scared me out of my wits**! My heart almost stopped.

A: キャーッ! 誰?
B: 僕だってば。
A: ヒャーッ、本当に怖かった! 心臓が止まるかと思ったわ。

63 That makes two of us.
私も同じ考えだ

A: Let's eat. I'm hungry.
B: **That makes two of us.**

A: 食べよう。お腹減った。
B: 僕もだ。

➜ 「そうすると(同じ考えの人間は)これで我々2人になった」という意味。ここでの make は Two and two make(s) four. (2たす2は4) と同じ用法。I feel the same way. と言うよりもややくだけた表現。なお、同意を表す方法としては次のようなものもある。語順に注意する必要がある。

A: I like old movies.

A: 私古い映画が好き。

B: That makes two of us.
or So do I. *or* Me, too.

B: 私も。

A: I can't believe it.
B: That makes two of us.
or Neither can I.
or I can't either.

A: 信じらんない。
B: 僕もだよ。

64 be (just) kidding
冗談を言う

A: I'm going to Hollywood to make horror movies.
B: Do you have a job?
A: I was just kidding. Did you really believe me?

A: ハリウッドに行って恐怖映画を作るんだ。
B: 仕事があるの？
A: 冗談だよ。本当に信じたの？

A: She won a car.
B: You're kidding! (*or* You **must be kidding**!)
A: No, I'm not. She really won a car!

A: あの子ね、賞品で車もらったのよ。
B: うそだろ？
A: 本当だってば。本当に車もらったんだから！

➡ You're kidding! は You must be joking. よりもややくだけた表現。

❖ You're pulling my leg.「冗談でしょう？」

A: There's going to be an earthquake tomorrow.
B: You're pulling my leg. No one knows when an earthquake will happen.
A: But I read it in the newspaper.

A: 明日地震があるんだよ。
B: からかってるんだろ。地震がいつ起きるかなんて誰にも分かるわけないじゃない。
A: だって新聞で読んだんだもん。

Are We Couch Potatoes?

65 move over

つめて場所をあける

A: Gail, could you please **move over** a little so someone else can sit down?
B: Oh, sorry. I didn't realize I was taking up so much space... Here—now you can sit down.

A: ゲイル、他に人が座れるように少しつめてくれる?
B: ああ、ごめんなさい。そんなに場所を取ってるなんて気がつかなかった。さあ、これで座れるでしょ?

❖ move *something* over (to a place) 「(何かを)移動させる」

A: If you **move** the couch **over** to the corner, I think the room will look better.
B: I'd rather **move** it **over** to the window. OK?

A: ソファーを隅のほうに動かしてくれればもっと部屋が見栄えすると思うけどな。
B: 窓のほうに動かしたらと思うけど、いいかな?

66 Here you go.

はい、どうぞ

A: **Here you go.** Can I get you anything else?
B: Yes. I'd like another cup of coffee.
A: Sure. I'll be right back.

A: はいっ、他に何か持ってきましょうか?
B: うん、もう一杯コーヒーが欲しいな。
A: わかった。すぐ戻ってくるわね。

A: Mom, can I have some more?
B: OK, but just a little. **Here you go.**

A: お母さん、もう少しちょうだい。
B: いいわ。でもちょっとだけよ。**はいどうぞ。**

➾ 人にものを手渡すときに用いる表現。Here you are. とほぼ同じで、親しい人どうしの会話に用いる。Here it is. はこれらよりややあらたまった感じ。

67 hit pause/play
一時停止／再生ボタンを押す

A: Can you **hit pause**? I need to make a quick phone call.
B: Now? Can't you wait 'til the end of the show?

A: OK I'm back. You can **hit play**.
B: I will in a minute, but first I'd like you to tell me why your "quick" call lasted 20 minutes.

A: ポーズのボタン押してくれる？ちょっと電話しなくちゃ。
B: 今？番組が終わるまで待てないの？

A: さあ戻ったよ。**再生ボタン押して。**
B: そりゃいいけど、それよりどうして「ちょっと」が20分になったりするわけ？

Are We Couch Potatoes?

68 a couch potato/couch potatoes
カウチ・ポテト族

A: Turn off the TV. You've been watching for six whole hours!
B: I know. I guess I'm **a couch potato**.

A: テレビ消せよ。もう6時間もずっと見てるんだよ。
B: わかってる。僕って**カウチ・ポテト族**なんだよね。

➜ ソファーでポテトなどのスナック菓子を食べながら長時間テレビばかり見ている人たちのこと。

69 Why do you ask?
なぜ(そんなことを)たずねるの?

A: How much money do you have with you?
B: **Why do you ask?**
A: I was just curious.

A: 今いくら持ってる?
B: 何でそんなこと?
A: ちょっと興味あっただけ。

70 spend (a little/a lot of) time (doing/on) *something*

～して(少し／たくさんの)時間を費やす

A: He **spends a lot of time** working. The kids never see him.
B: Then it's time for a change, isn't it?

A: 彼は仕事ばっかりしていて子供にも会う時間がないのよ。
B: じゃあそろそろ生活変えたほうがいいかもね。

A: You need to **spend more time on** your homework, don't you think?
B: I guess so.

A: 君ね、もっと宿題に時間をかけないといけないとは思わないか？
B: そうだね。

71 be glued to the TV/tube

テレビに釘付け

A: Bobby. Dinner's ready!
B: He doesn't seem to hear you.
A: I know. He's always **glued to the tube**. Listen—he won't hear this: Bobby ... the house is on fire! See—he still didn't hear me.

A: ボビー、夕ご飯できたわよ！
B: ちっとも聞いてないようだね。
A: そうね。いつもテレビに釘付けなんだから。ねえ、これでもきっと聞いてないわよ。ボビー... 火事よー！ほらね、まだ聞こえてないんだから。

Are We Couch Potatoes?

72 That's funny.

□□

変だぞ

A: **That's funny.** I thought I left my keys on the table, but they're nowhere to be seen.
B: Here they are. They fell.

A: **おかしいな。**テーブルの上にカギ置いたと思ったんだけど、どこにもないんだ。
B: はいこれ。落ちたんだよ。

A: 20… 25… 26… 27… I only have $27 in my wallet. **That's funny.** Yesterday I had $100 and I don't remember spending that much.
B: Didn't you go out to dinner last night?
A: Yeah, but I didn't spend $70!

A: 20… 25… 26… 27… 財布に27ドルしかないぞ。**変だなあ。**昨日100ドルあってそんなにたくさん使ったはずないんだけど。
B: 昨日の晩は夕食に出かけなかった？
A: うん、行ったけど70ドルも使ってないよ！

➸ That's strange/unusual. とも言う。「面白い、おかしい」の意味で用いられている次の例と対比する。

❖ That … is funny.「あの～は面白い」

A: **That** movie **is** really **funny**. You should see it.
B: I think I will. I need a good laugh.

A: あの映画、本当に**おかしい**よ。見れば？
B: そうしよっと。思いっきり笑いたいの。

73 be a bookworm
本の虫だ

A: Let's go for a walk.
B: Not now. I'm in the middle of this great book.
A: You're such **a bookworm**. Every time I look at you, you've got a book in your hands.

A: 散歩行こうよ。
B: 今はだめ。このすばらしい本を読んでるんだから。
A: あなたって本当にすごい**本の虫**よね。いつ見ても何か本を持ってるんだから。

74 put (a book) down
読むのをやめる

A: Dinner's ready.
B: Start without me. I can't **put this book down**.

A: 夕ご飯できたわよ。
B: 先に食べてて。この**本やめられない**んだ。

A: Why do you look so tired?
B: I didn't sleep last night. I was reading a book that I couldn't **put down** until I finished it.

A: どうしてそんなに疲れた顔してるの?
B: 昨日の晩寝れなかったんだ。本を読んでて終わるまで**やめられなかった**もんだから。

➜ 手に持って読んでいる本を「下に置く」ことから stop reading の語義が生じてくる。具体的、物理的な意味から発展的な意味を理解することが大切。

Are We Couch Potatoes?

75 be/get involved in

のめり込む

A: Why don't you turn the TV off?
B: Because I'**m involved in** this show. I'll turn it off when the show's over.

A: テレビなんで消さないの？
B: この番組にすっかりハマッちゃって。終わったら消すよ。

A: I thought you were reading that book.
B: I was, but I put it down. I **couldn't get involved in** it.

A: 例の本読んでるのかと思ったのに。
B: 読んでたんだけどやめたんだ。なかなか入り込んでいけなくて。

❖ be involved with *someone* 「異性とつき合う」

A: **Are** you **involved with anyone** now?
B: Why do you ask?

A: 君誰かつきあってる人いるの？
B: なぜそんなこと聞くのよ？

→ もともと be involved は「かかわりあいになる」という意味で、ここから He is involved in playing Nintendo.「テレビゲームに夢中だ」のように、「熱中する」という意味合いを持つようになった。異性と付き合うということは相手に「熱中」することなのでこの言いまわしが用いられる。be going out with とほぼ同じ意味で、keep company with よりも口語的。

e·x·e·r·c·i·s·e·s

1) テープ(CD)を聴いて、次のダイアローグの空欄に適当な語句を書き入れてみましょう。

JACK: I'm bored.
JILL: So am I. What do you (1)_____ doing?
JACK: We could watch TV.
JILL: No. Remember, we promised each other that we'd watch only an hour a day. You don't want to become (2)_____, do you?
JACK: I don't want to (3)_____ reading, either.
JILL: So, watch a little TV and read a little, too.
JACK: And what will I do with the rest of my time?
JILL: (4)_____ getting some more exercise?
JACK: I'm never (5)_____ to exercise.
JILL: (6)_____, but we should force ourselves to take an exercise class.
JACK: (7)_____!
JILL: No, I'm not. I'm serious. People our age get heart attacks and it (8)_____. We need to get more exercise.
JACK: (9)_____ I never thought I'd hear you say that.
JILL: Well, I saw some shows on TV about the importance of exercise, and…
JACK: Oh, so you were watching daytime TV???
JILL: But…

Are We Couch Potatoes? • 95

e·x·e·r·c·i·s·e·s

2 次の1～14の文に対する返答として適当なものを97ページのa～nより選んでみましょう。

____ 1. Come in and make yourselves comfortable.
____ 2. I'd like two tickets, please.
____ 3. We got married last week.
____ 4. Let's get together for coffee.
____ 5. I feel like getting some exercise.
____ 6. Can you hit pause for a second?
____ 7. Were you ever involved with each other?
____ 8. She's an hour late.
____ 9. You're shaking.
____10. Your eyes are red.
____11. Want to dance?
____12. I need a vacation.
____13. It's kind of crowded here.
____14. Put down that book and listen to me!

a. Where's the remote?
b. Why do you ask?
c. That car scared me out of my wits.
d. You're kidding!
e. Get your bike and I'll meet you at the park.
f. Sorry. I'm not in the mood right now.
g. Sorry. I was involved.
h. Where should we put our coats?
i. Great idea. How's tomorrow?
j. That's funny. She's always on time. Let's give her a call.
k. Here you go.
l. That makes two of us.
m. I just saw a tearjerker. There wasn't a dry eye in the house.
n. I'll move over.

Lesson 5 Answer Key

Exercise 1
1. feel like
2. a couch potato
3. spend all my time
4. How about
5. in the mood
6. That makes two of us
7. You're kidding
8. scares me out of my wits
9. That's funny

Exercise 2

1. h	2. k	3. d	4. i	5. e	6. a
7. b	8. j	9. c	10. m	11. f	12. l
13. n	14. g				

Forgetting a Date

デートをすっぽかす

Lesson 6

D·I·A·L·O·G·U·E

BOB: Nancy! Uh-oh! Nancy... wait!
NANCY: Why should I?
BOB: Listen, I'm really embarrassed about last night. **To be honest with you**, I completely forgot about our date.
NANCY: I know.
BOB: I didn't mean to **hurt your feelings**.
NANCY: But you did. Obviously I **wasn't on your mind**. You **stood me up**, Bob!
BOB: Listen, we can **work this out**. Let me **make up for** it. I'll **treat you to dinner** tonight.
NANCY: Aren't you going to explain what happened?
BOB: I did explain. I forgot to **show up**.
NANCY: Would YOU **stand for** an explanation like that?
BOB: Well, I guess **you've got a point there**. OK. Sit down, and I'll tell you the truth about what happened.

ボブ: ナンシー！ おーい、ナンシーったら、待ってくれ!
ナンシー: 何であんたなんか待たなきゃいけないのよ!
ボブ: ねえ、昨日の晩は本当に悪かったよ。本当のこと言うと、すっかりデートの約束忘れてたんだ。
ナンシー: そうみたいね。
ボブ: 君の気持ちを傷つけるつもりじゃなかったんだ。
ナンシー: そんなこと言ったってだめよ。私なんかどうでもいってこれではっきりしたわね。あなたにすっぽかされたんだもの、ボブ!
ボブ: ねえ、これ何とかできるんじゃないかな。この埋め合わせはするからさ。今夜は夕食ごちそうするよ。
ナンシー: 事情を説明してくれないわけ?
ボブ: したじゃないか。忘れてて来れなかったんだよ。
ナンシー: あなた、自分だったらそんな説明で納得できる?
ボブ: うん、そうだよね。わかった。座ってよ、何があったか本当のこと話すから。

➻ **2. Why should I?** 後にwaitが省略されていると考える。
　8. But you did. But you did hurt my feelings.の省略。ここでdidは強調のために用いられている。

Forgetting a Date • 101

76 to be honest with you/ to tell you the truth

本当のことを言うと

A: What time should we leave?
B: To be honest with you, I don't want to go.

A: What's the matter?
B: To tell you the truth, I don't love you any more.

A: いつごろ出かけましょうか?
B: 本当のこと言うと行きたくないんだ。

A: どうしたの?
B: 正直言って、もう君のこと愛してないんだ。

→ 通常あまり良くないことを言い出すときに用いられる表現。

77 hurt *someone's* feelings

気持ちを傷つける

A: I can't believe you didn't call me.
B: I'm sorry that/if **I hurt your feelings**.

A: 電話してくれなかったなんて信じらんない!
B: 気持ちを傷つけて悪かったよ。/気分を害したのなら謝るよ。

78 be on *someone's* mind

気にかかっている

A: I'm in love!
B: How can you be sure?
A: I can't stop thinking

A: 惚れたぞ!
B: どうしてわかるの?
A: 彼女のことばかり考えてる

102 • Lesson 6

about her. She's **on my mind** twenty-four hours a day!

んだ。24時間あの娘が**頭から離れない**んだよ。

❖ **have *something* on one's mind**「〜を気にかけている」

A: Why do you look so serious?
B: I **have** a lot **on my mind**.

A: そんなに深刻な顔してどうしたの？
B: **心配事がたくさんある**んだよ。

➥ 心配事などに用いられることが多い。

79 stand *someone* up
すっぽかす

A: She said she would meet me at 7:00, and it's already 9:00. I'm so angry!
B: Maybe something happened to make her late.
A: No, she didn't even call! She **stood me up**!

A: 彼女7時に会おうって言ってたのにもう9時だぞ、頭きた！
B: たぶん何かあって遅くなったんだと思うよ。
A: 違うよ。電話もしてこないんだから。あいつすっぽかしやがったんだ！

❖ **be stood up**「すっぽかされる」

A: Why is he so upset?
B: He **was stood up**.

A: 何で彼はあんなに怒ってるの？
B: **待ちぼうけくらわされた**んだよ。

➥ 異性とのデートに用いる表現。相手を立たせたままにしておくことから「すっぽかす」の意味に用いられる。

80 work *something* out

(問題などを)解決する

- **A:** Won't you please talk to me? As the Beatles said, "We can **work it out**."
- **B:** Maybe the Beatles can **work out** their problems, but can we?

- **A:** 頼むから口きいてくれないかい? ビートルズも言ってるじゃない、「何とかなるさ」って。
- **B:** ビートルズは何とかなっても私たちはどうかしらね。

➨ solve a problem よりも口語的な表現。

81 make up for

〜の埋め合わせをする

- **A:** You're not doing your share of the work. I've cooked dinner every night this week.
- **B:** I'm really sorry. Tell me how I can **make up for** it.
- **A:** You can **make up for** it by cooking dinner every night next week!

- **A:** あなた自分のするべきことちゃんとしてないわよ。今週は私が毎日夕食作ったんだから。
- **B:** 本当にごめん。どうやって**埋め合わせ**すればいいかな、言ってくれよ。
- **A:** 来週は毎日晩ご飯作ってくれたら**許してあげる**!

❖ make up 「仲直りする」、「作り上げる、でっちあげる」

- **A:** Are Jack and Jill together again?
- **B:** Yes, they **made up** last

- **A:** ジャックとジルはよりが戻ったの?
- **B:** うん、先週**仲直り**したん

104 • Lesson 6

week.

A: Did she get in trouble for being late?
B: Nope (No). She **made up** an interesting story/excuse about why she was late.

A: あの子遅れてひどいめにあったのかな？
B: ううん。何かおもしろい言い訳をでっちあげたみたいよ。

❖ **makeup** 「化粧、メーキャップ」

A: Go wash your face! You're wearing too much **makeup** for a girl your age.
B: But, Dad—everyone wears **makeup**!

A: 顔洗って来い！お前くらいの歳の女の子にしちゃケバイぞ、**お化粧**が濃いぞ。
B: でもお父さん、**お化粧**ぐらい誰でもしてるわよ！

82 treat *someone* (to *something*)

おごる

A: I'll pay for dinner tonight.
B: Come on. Let me **treat you** to dinner.
A: I wanted to **treat YOU**!
B: You can **treat me** next time.

A: 今晩は夕食私が払うわ。
B: いいわよ、私に**おごらせ**て。
A: あなたに**おごって**あげようと思ってたのよ。
B: じゃ今度お願いする(**おごってもらう**)わ。

➥ 食事代や入場券などの料金を他人のために払うこと。こういった場合には It's on me. あるいは I'll get it. とも言える。割り勘にしたいときは Let's split it. という(Lesson 7 参照)。

Forgetting a Date • 105

83 show up

現れる、やって来る

A: Why is Diane in trouble with Sam?
B: His party started at 9:00 and she **showed up** at 11:30!

A: ダイアンはどうしてサムともめてるの?
B: サムたちのパーティは9時からだったのに彼女が**現れ**たのが11時半だったの!

A: Why are you home so early?
B: My teacher **didn't show up**, and we didn't have a substitute.

A: 何で帰りがこんなに早いの?
B: 先生が**来なくて**、それに代講もなかったんだ。

➻ arrive, appear よりも口語的な表現。

84 (not) stand for *something*

我慢する(しない)

A: I'm afraid I'm going to fail this test.
B: I know you're worried, but don't try to cheat. The teacher won't **stand for** cheating.

A: 今度のテスト落としちゃいそうだ。
B: 心配なのは分かるけど、ズルしちゃだめだよ。先生はカンニング**には厳しい**ぞ。

➻ 名詞・動名詞が目的語となる。

❖ can't stand「嫌いだ、我慢できない」

A: I hope it snows. I love the winter.
B: Not me. **I can't stand** cold weather. /to be cold. /being cold.

A: 雪だといいな。冬って大好き。
B: 僕はダメ。寒いのは**嫌**だよ。

➤ 名詞・不定詞・動名詞が目的語となる。

85 You've got a point (there).
それはそうだね

A: I think we should take the train to the mountains.
B: I'd rather drive.
A: But there's going to be a lot of snow.
B: I like snow.
A: Do you like sitting in the car for hours, stuck in the snow?
B: You've got a point there. Let's take the train.

A: 山まで電車で行ったほうがいいと思うな。
B: 車のほうがいいわ。
A: でも雪がすごいよ、きっと。
B: 雪好きだもん。
A: 雪で身動きとれなくて車に何時間も座ることになってもいいのかい？
B: **そう言われればそうよね。**電車にしましょうか。

➤ 「あなたの言うことはその点については認めざるをえない」というニュアンスで、譲歩するときに用いる。

Forgetting a Date • 107

e·x·e·r·c·i·s·e·s

1) テープ(CD)を聴いて、次のダイアローグの空欄に適当な語句を書き入れてみましょう。

LAWYER: You must tell the truth here. If you don't, you'll go to prison.

NANCY: I'm not lying to you. I'm not (1)_____ stories. I did not kill Bob. (2)_____ , I don't know why I'm here.

LAWYER: Because you were seen talking to him right before the murder. What were you talking about?

NANCY: He was embarrassed about forgetting our date and he was trying to (3)_____ . But I was still angry.

LAWYER: Why?

NANCY: He wasn't telling me the real reason why he (4)_____ . I told him that I wouldn't (5)_____ his simple explanation. I (6)_____ being lied to.

LAWYER: So you killed him.

NANCY: I did not! Finally, he did explain why he didn't (7)_____ the night before.

LAWYER: Well?

108 • Lesson 6

NANCY: You're really embarrassing me. OK. He said that he had met his old girlfriend unexpectedly and (8)_____ to dinner.

LAWYER: Aha! So you were jealous and wanted to kill him!

NANCY: Only for a minute. We sat down and talked. He knew he had (9)_____ and he apologized. We both wanted to (10)_____ because we loved each other. Why don't you talk to his ex-girlfriend? She was probably more jealous than I was!

LAWYER: (11)_____.

e·x·e·r·c·i·s·e·s

2 次の1〜13の文に対する返答として適当なものを111ページのa〜mより選んでみましょう。

_____ 1. Why are you so upset?
_____ 2. What do you have on your face?
_____ 3. Look! They're laughing together. I thought they had a fight.
_____ 4. How can I make up for what I did?
_____ 5. I was absent for no reason. What should I tell the teacher?
_____ 6. Why did you treat him?
_____ 7. What time should I show up?
_____ 8. Why didn't you come to my party?
_____ 9. Talk to me. We can work this out.
_____ 10. I'll pick you up at 8:00.
_____ 11. Why do you look so worried?
_____ 12. Why isn't she paying attention?
_____ 13. He's late all the time.

a. Make up an excuse.
b. They made up.
c. By 6:00.
d. It was his birthday.
e. You hurt my feelings.
f. All right. What should we do?
g. To be honest with you, I was too tired.
h. Makeup.
i. I have a lot on my mind.
j. Just tell me you're sorry.
k. Don't stand me up!
l. I wouldn't stand for that kind of behavior.
m. She has Bob on her mind.

LESSON 6 **Answer Key**

Exercise 1
1. making up
2. To be honest with you
3. make up
4. stood me up
5. stand for
6. can't stand
7. show up
8. treated her
9. hurt my feelings
10. work it out
11. You've got a point there

Exercise 2
1. e	2. h	3. b	4. j	5. a	6. d
7. c	8. g	9. f	10. k	11. i	12. m
13. l					

For Here or to Go?

こちらでお召し上がりですか、お持ち帰りですか?

Lesson 7

D·I·A·L·O·G·U·E

MOLLIE: The line sure is long.

RONNIE: Well, we're not in a hurry. What are you going to... Did you see that? That guy **cut in line**.

MOLLIE: I can't believe people like that. It's a good thing we're not in a hurry. Anyway, lunch **is on me** today.

RONNIE: Uh-uh. **It's my turn.**

MOLLIE: No, it isn't! You treat me every time we **eat out**.

RONNIE: Why don't we compromise and **split it** then?

MOLLIE: Because I'm treating you, and **that's that**.

....

MOLLIE: One hamburger, one chicken sandwich, two small fries, and two cokes.

COUNTERPERSON: Is that **for here or to go**?

MOLLIE: For here.

....

モリー:	本当に長い列ね。
ロニー:	まあね、でもそんなに急いでるわけでもないし。さあ、何を... あれ見たかい? あいつ列に割り込んだぞ。
モリー:	ああいう人って信じらんない。急いでないからいいようなもんだけどね。とにかく今日のお昼は私に出させてね。
ロニー:	だめだよ、僕の番だよ。
モリー:	違うわ、外で食べるときいつもおごってもらってるでしょ。
ロニー:	じゃ、間をとってワリカンにしようか。
モリー:	私がおごるって言ってるんだから本当にいいのよ。

・・・・・・・・・・

モリー:	ハンバーガーひとつ、チキン・サンドイッチひとつ、フライド・ポテトの小ふたつ、それとコーラふたつお願いします。
店員:	こちらで召し上がりますか、お持ち帰りですか?
モリー:	ここで食べます。

・・・・・・・・・・

D·I·A·L·O·G·U·E

MOLLIE: Do you know what Casey **is up to** these days?
RONNIE: **You got me.**
MOLLIE: He's **taking a** quit-smoking **class**.
RONNIE: **It's about time.** He's the only one I know who still smokes.
MOLLIE: Ronnie, **don't be so hard on** him. You know he's tried almost everything—gum, hypnosis. He's even **gone cold turkey**.
RONNIE: I hope he... **Look who's here** ... Hey, Casey! Over here!
MOLLIE: **Speak of the devil!**
CASEY: Were you talking about me?
MOLLIE: Yeah, I was telling Ronnie about the class you're taking.
CASEY: Well, that's no secret. I **figure** if I tell everyone I know that I'm taking that class, they won't let me smoke.
RONNIE: Not a bad idea. **How's it going?**
CASEY: Pretty well **so far**. I**'ve got a long way**

モリー: 最近ケーシーどうしてるか知ってる?
ロニー: 見当つかないな。
モリー: 禁煙クラスに出てるのよ。
ロニー: そういうことがあってもいい頃だな。僕の知ってる人でタバコをまだ吸ってるのは彼だけだよ。
モリー: ロニーったら、あんまり彼のことひどく言わないで。あの人ほとんど何でもやってみたんだから。ガムも催眠法も、いきなりスパッと禁煙したりもしたんだから。
ロニー: あいつもこれでさ... おっと誰かと思ったら... おーい、ケーシー! こっちだよ!
モリー: 噂をすれば影ってやつね!
ケーシー: 僕のこと話してたの?
モリー: そうよ、ロニーにあなたが出てる禁煙クラスのこと。
ケーシー: ああ、あれは秘密でも何でもないし。あのクラスに出てるって言っちゃえばみんな僕に吸わせないようにしてくれるだろうって思うしね。
ロニー: 悪くない思いつきだ。で、どうなの?

D·I·A·L·O·G·U·E

to go. But I've **made a promise to** myself. I'm not going to **give up** this time—I'm not going to **end up** be**ing** the only smoker in this town.

ケーシー: 今のとこ快調だよ。先は長いって感じだけどね。でも自分自身に約束したんだ。今度はあきらめないぞって。この町でひとりだけタバコ吸ってるなんてことにならないように。

➜ **1. The line sure is long.** surely, certainly のくだけた形。The line is certainly long. よりも感情がこもっている感じ。
32. tell A about B で「AにBのことを話す」の意味。

86 cut in line

列に割り込む

A: Let's **cut in line** to make sure that we get into the theater.
B: No way. How can you even think of doing that? I'm going to the back of the line.

A: ちゃんと入場できるようにちょっと**割り込んじゃおう**か。
B: 絶対ダメ。よくもそんなこと考えつくわね。私は列の後ろにつくわ。

❖ **get in line**「列の後ろに並ぶ」

A: Why don't you **get in line** while I park the car?
B: Good idea.

A: 僕が車とめてる間に**並んで**てよ。
B: それがいいね。

➺ get on lineと言うこともある。

87 (It's) on me.

私が払います

A: Dinner **is on me** tonight.
B: No, you shouldn't...
A: No argument. It's my pleasure.
B: Thank you.

A: 今夜は夕食**僕が出す**よ。
B: だめよ、そんな...
A: いいったらいいの。そうしたいんだ。
B: ありがとう。

➺ こう言われたときは一応最初は断り、その後で相手の申し出を受け入れて感謝するというのが普通。

88 Let's split it/the check/the tab./Let's go Dutch.

割り勘にしよう

A: Let me treat you. (*or* It's on me.)
B: No, **let's split it**. This restaurant is so expensive.
  or **Let's split the check.**
  or **Let's split the tab.**
  or **Let's go Dutch.**
A: All right, but let me pay the tip.

A: 僕が払うよ。
B: いいえ、**割り勘にしましょう**。このお店とても高いわ。
A: わかったよ。でもチップは僕にまかせて。

➽ Let's split. という表現は Let's leave. の意味で若者が使うことがある。この場合はお金の支払いとは関係がないので注意。なお、これはかなりくだけた表現で、ごく親しい友達同士で用いられる。

89 It's my turn (to)

私の番です、私が〜する番です

A: **It's my turn to** drive, so I'll pick you up.
B: I'll be waiting for you on the corner.

A: 今度は僕が運転する番だ。迎えに行くよ。
B: 角のところで待ってるね。

❖ **take turns —ing** 「交代で〜する」

A: It's a long trip, so we should **take turns** driv**ing**, don't you think?
B: Absolutely.

A: 長距離だから**代わりばんこ**に運転したほうがいいよね？
B: まったくそのとおり。

For Here or to Go?

90 eat out

外食する

A: Let's **eat out** tonight.
B: Great idea. How about Chinese food?

A: 今日は**外で食べましょう**よ。
B: いいね。中華なんてどう?

❖ **go out to eat**「食事に出かける」

- Let's **go out to eat** tonight. I don't feel like cooking.
- 今夜は外食しよう。料理する気がしないや。

91 That's that./That's final.

もうこれで決まりだ

A (child): I want to go to the movies.
B (child): I want to go to the park.
C (parent): We're going to go home, and **that's that**.

A: 映画に行きたいよ。
B: 公園に行こうよ。
C: 家に帰るのよ、いいわねっ。

➜「もう結論は出ているので話し合いの余地はない」という意味なので、大人に対してこの表現を使うのはレストランで相手におごってあげるときなど、好意を示す場合に限ったほうが無難。

92 For here or to go?

こちらでお召し上がりですか、お持ち帰りですか

A: **For here or to go?**
B: **To go**, please.

A: こちらでお召し上がりですか、お持ち帰りですか。
B: 持ち帰ります。

➜ ファースト・フードの店で用いる決まり文句。Is this to go? とも言う。

93 be up to
〜をしている、しようとしている

- **A:** What **are** you **up to**?
- **B:** Nothing much. Just the regular routine.

- **A:** 今どうしてるの?
- **B:** 別に。いつもと同じだよ。

- **A:** What **are** you **up to**?
- **B:** Spring cleaning. It's a big job.

- **A:** 今何してるの。
- **B:** 春の掃除。大仕事だ。

❖ not be up to —ing 「〜する元気がない」

- **A:** Let's go.
- **B:** I'm going to stay home. I'm **not up to** go**ing** out. I'm too tired.

- **A:** 行こう。
- **B:** 僕は家にいる。とても出かける気がしないよ。とっても疲れてるんだ。

❖ What's up? 「どうしてる?」「どうしたの?」

- **A:** Hi, Casey! **What's up?**
- **B:** Nothing much. I'm still taking that class.

- **A:** やあ、ケーシー! どうしてる?
- **B:** 別に。まだ例のクラスに出てるよ。

– Mollie, you look really upset. **What's up?**
(What's the matter?)

– モリー、ずいぶん焦ってるみたいだけど、どうかしたの?

➜ What's happening? What's new? What's the matter? などの表現とほぼ同じ意味で用いられる。

94 You('ve) got me.

分からない

A: Where's the dog?
B: **You got me.**

A: 犬はどこ行った？
B: わかんない。

➜ ここでの get は「(人を)困らせる、やり込める」の意味で、This question gets me. (この質問には弱った)のように使う。I have no idea. I don't know. よりもかなりくだけた表現なので相当親しい友達や家族などの他は避けたほうが無難。

95 take a class/classes

授業を取る

A: What are you **taking** this semester?
B: English, math, history, and biology.
A: I'm **taking** two P.E. (physical education) **classes** this semester, and they're a lot of fun.
B: What are you **taking**?
A: Tennis and swimming.

A: 今学期は何取ってるの？
B: 英語、数学、歴史、それと生物。
A: 今学期は体育の**クラス**ふたつ取ってるんだ。とっても楽しいよ。
B: 何やってるの？
A: テニスと水泳。

❖ take a test / take tests 「試験を受ける」

– Whenever I **take a test**, I get really nervous.
– When you **take tests**, be sure to keep your eyes on your own paper.

– **試験を受ける**ときっていつも緊張してしまうんだ。
– **試験を受ける**ときは、自分の試験用紙だけを見ているように。

96 It's about time (that)

〜てもいい頃だ

A: The bus is finally here, and **it's about time**. Twenty minutes late!
B: Next time, let's drive instead.

A: It's about time that she stopped smoking. She should have stopped a long time ago.
B: She tried, but she couldn't.

A: やっとバスが来たぞ。もう来てもいい頃だよね、20分も遅れてるんだからさ！
B: 今度は車で行こうよ。

A: あの人ももうタバコやめてもいい頃だよね。本当はずっと前にやめてるべきだったんだ。
B: 努力はしたんだけどできなかったんだよ。

➸ 多少いらだちや怒りの気持ちがこもる感じ。

97 Don't be so hard on *someone*

そんなにつらく当たらないで

A (father): You're late again. It's 2:00 a.m. and you were supposed to be home by midnight.
B (son or daughter): Sorry, Dad. I didn't have my watch.
A (father): That's no excuse. You're not going out again at night for a month.
C (mother): Don't be so hard on him/her! A month is a long time.

A: お前また遅いぞ。もう夜中の2時だぞ。12時までには帰ってくるはずだったろ？
B: ごめんなさい、お父さん。時計持ってなかったんだ／なかったのよ。
A: そんなの言い訳になってない。これから1ヵ月は夜外出させないからな。
C: そんなにきつく言わなくても。1ヵ月は長すぎるわ。

➜ Don't be so mean/strict. とほぼ同じ。

98 quit/go cold turkey

やめる

A: Maybe you should try to smoke a little less every day.
B: That won't work. **I have to quit cold turkey**. I'm going to throw this pack of cigarettes into the garbage right now

A: たぶん毎日少しずつ吸う量を減らしていけばいいんじゃないかな。
B: それじゃだめだよ。思いきってスパッとやめないと。たった今このタバコを箱ごとゴミ箱に捨てて、もう一生二度と1本も吸わない

126 • Lesson 7

and never smoke another cigarette again in my life.

A: Are you going to go to a quit smoking class?
B: No, I'm going to **go cold turkey** without any help.

ぞ。

A: 禁煙クラスに行くつもり？
B: いいや、人の助けを借りないで**ピタッと**やめるんだ。

➻ タバコや酒などを、徐々にではなくいきなりスパッとやめること。stop doing something suddenly and completely よりも生き生きとした感じ。

99 Look who's here!

誰かと思った!

- **Look who's here!** I can't believe it! It's great to see you.

- 誰かと思った！信じられないよ！会えて嬉しいな。

➥ Look at who just arrived. よりも意外性・驚きの感情がこもっている感じがする表現。

100 Speak of the devil!

噂をすれば影

A: Jennifer is going to be famous some day. She really is a great actress.

B: I know. And she can sing, too. Have you ever heard her?

A: ジェニファーはいまに有名になるわよ。本当にすばらしい女優さんなんだから。

B: そうよね。それに歌だって歌えるし。聞いたことある？

A: Oh, yes. About a year ago... **Speak of the devil!** There she is. Should we invite her to join us?

A: ええ、一年ぐらい前かなあ… **噂をすれば影ってやつね**、ほら、ご本人の登場よ。声かけてご一緒しましょうか?

➸ 他人の噂話をしている最中に本人が現れたときの決まり文句。Speak of the Devil, and he is sure to appear.「悪魔の話をすれば悪魔が現れる」ということわざに由来する。会話ではand 以下の部分を言わないのが普通。

101 figure

思う、判断する、信じる

□□

A: I **figure**, if I save $50 a month. I still won't have enough to travel.

B: Try to save $100. You can do it.

A: ひと月に50ドル貯めたとして、それでもまだ旅行するには足りないと**思う**な。

B: じゃ100ドル貯めれば。君ならできるよ。

➸ think よりもより口語的。

102 How's it going?

うまくいってる?

A: I just started swimming every day.
B: How's it going?
A: Pretty well.

A: 毎日泳ぐの、始めたの。
B: で、どう?
A: バッチリ。

A: I'm finally taking a computer class.
B: How's it going?

A: ついにパソコンのクラスに通ってるの。
B: うまくいってる?

➜ 習い事などの上達ぐあいを訊ねるためのくだけた表現。Are you making progress in what you already started? ということ。また、相手の健康状態を訊ねる場合にも用いることがある。How are you? よりもくだけた感じ。次の会話を参照すること。

A: Hi! **How's it going?**
B: Not bad. How are you?

A: やあ、調子はどう?
B: 悪くないね。君は?

103 so far

これまでは、そこまでは

A: How do you like the book?
B: I've only read a few pages. **So far** I think I like it, but I'm not really sure.

A: その本、気に入った?
B: まだほんのちょっとしか読んでないんだ。今のところ気に入ってるけど、まだ分からないね。

➜ until now, up to a point とほぼ同じ。

❖ **so far, so good**「ここまではまあまあだ、それまではよろしい」

A: How's the book?
B: So far, so good.

A: その本、どう？
B: 今のところいいみたい。

104 have (got) a long way to go
先は長い

A: You've made a lot of progress so far.
B: Thanks a lot, but I **have a long way to go**.

A: 今までずいぶん上達したよね。
B: ありがとう。でもまだ先は長いよ。

➡ 「目的地までまだずいぶん距離がある」というのが文字通りの意味で、ここから「目的を達するまではまだまだずいぶん努力が必要だ」という解釈が生じてくる。

105 make a promise/promises (to *someone*)

約束する

A: She always **makes promises** that she doesn't keep.
B: I know what you mean. It's hard to trust what she says.

A: 彼女は約束しても守ったためしがないんだ。
B: わかるわ。あの子の言うことなんて信用できないわよね。

❖ **keep a promise**「約束を守る」, **break a promise**「約束を破る」

A: I promise that I will do my homework every night. and that I will do it well.
B: I hope that you will **keep your promise**.
A: I never **break a promise**. Believe me.

A: 毎晩宿題するよ、ちゃんとやるから。約束するよ。
B: **約束は守ってよね**。
A: 僕は**約束破ったりしない**よ。信じてよ。

106 give up

あきらめる、やめる

A: I **give up**! I can't do it. I've been practicing pronunciation every day and people still don't understand me.
B: Don't **give up** so fast. You need to be more patient.

A: やーめた！できないや。毎日ずっと発音の練習してるのに僕の言うことまだ通じないんだ。
B: そんなにすぐあきらめたらだめだよ。もっと辛抱しなきゃ。

132 • Lesson 7

❖ **give up (*something*)**「〜をやめる」

A: They are going to **give up** smoking so their children won't imitate them.
B: That's good to hear.

A: あの人達ね、子供が真似しないようにタバコをやめるんだって。
B: それはいいことだね。

107 end up —ing
結局最後には〜する、〜になる

– She's really interested in biology. I bet she'll **end up** becom**ing** a doctor.

– At the party we started out being nervous, but we **ended up** hav**ing** fun.

– We were going to go to the movies, but we **ended up** go**ing** out to eat.

– They started out happy but **ended up** gett**ing** a divorce.

– At first he loved his job, but he **ended up** hat**ing** it.

– At first she hated her job, but she **ended up** lov**ing** it.

― 彼女は生物が本当に面白いみたいだね。**お医者さんにでもなっちゃうよ、きっと。**

― 僕らパーティで最初のうちは緊張してたんだけど、**しまいには結構楽しめたよ。**

― 映画に行こうと思ってたんだけど、**結局外で食事する**ことにしたの。

― 二人は最初幸せだったけど、**結局は離婚さ。**

― 彼は最初仕事が気に入っていたけど、**しまいには嫌気がさしたみたい。**

― 彼女は初めのうちは仕事が嫌だったけど、**後になって好きになったの。**

➥ 良いことにも悪いことにも使われる。

For Here or to Go?

e·x·e·r·c·i·s·e·s

1 テープ(CD)を聴いて、次のダイアローグの空欄に適当な語句を書き入れてみましょう。

CHERYL: I'm so glad I'm (1)_____
I (2)_____ to myself to come here at least five times a week.

KATE: That often? You'll (3)_____ with big muscles!

CHERYL: I just want to be healthy. I (4)_____ if I come here a lot, the exercises will become easier for me. Hey—(5)_____—Virginia—are you taking a class here?

VIRGINIA: Hi, (6)_____?

CHERYL: Fine. Are you taking a class here?

VIRGINIA: I'm not really sure. I was just taking a look. How is the class?

CHERYL: (7)_____. We've had only two classes, and my muscles really hurt.

KATE: Mine do, too, but it feels good. Listen, why don't we go out for lunch. Are you free?

CHERYL: I'm free, but I can't (8)_____ because I'm trying to save money.

KATE: No problem. (9)_____.

CHERYL: Thanks, Kate, but I really have a lot to do any-

way this afternoon. Maybe some other time.
KATE: How about you, Virginia?
VIRGINIA: I'll be free around one. Do you want to meet at the deli?

e·x·e·r·c·i·s·e·s

次の **1〜18** の文に対する返答として適当なものを137ページの **a〜r** より選んでみましょう。

_____ 1. It's on me.
_____ 2. For here or to go?
_____ 3. Let's cut in line.
_____ 4. You never do anything right.
_____ 5. Look who's here!
_____ 6. Remember Andrea and Gregory?
_____ 7. How's it going?
_____ 8. Doctor, will he be OK?
_____ 9. Have you seen Bill? He cut his hair.
_____ 10. Let me ride the bike a little longer.
_____ 11. Here comes the waitress.
_____ 12. What's Aaron doing today?
_____ 13. Come on. Just one more time.
_____ 14. Let's split. I'm tired.
_____ 15. I think we eat out too much.
_____ 16. The baby's too quiet.
_____ 17. I can't do it.
_____ 18. How does this thing work?

a. Don't be so hard on me.
b. Yeah, I heard they ended up getting married.
c. So far, so good.
d. Speak of the devil! There he is right now!
e. It's about time. We've been sitting here for 20 minutes.
f. I know. We'd better see what she's up to.
g. Amy and Kirk—It's great to see you!
h. You got me!
i. Yes. He's made a lot of progress. But he's still got a long way to go.
j. No—let's split it.
k. No way, I hate when people do that to me.
l. Yeah, it's getting expensive.
m. He's taking a computer class.
n. I said no, and that's that!
o. No! It's my turn.
p. Don't give up. Try again.
q. Me, too.
r. To go, please.

LESSON 7 **Answer Key**

Exercise 1

1. taking this class
2. made a promise
3. end up
4. figure
5. look who's here
6. how's it going?
7. So far, so good
8. eat out
9. It's on me

Exercise 2

1. j	2. r	3. k	4. a	5. g
6. b	7. c	8. i	9. d	
10. o (*or* n)	11. e	12. m	13. n	14. q
15. l	16. f	17. p	18. h	

How About Going to a Movie?

映画に行くのはどう?

Lesson

8

D·I·A·L·O·G·U·E

ROSEMARY: Hello?

FRANK: Hi, Rosemary. This is Frank. How're you doing?

ROSEMARY: OK, but busy.

FRANK: Can you **make time to** go to a movie this afternoon?

ROSEMARY: I wish I could. but I have a lot of homework. I'll have to **take a rain check**.

FRANK: Come on, **take** some **time off**. You're always studying! You're going to **turn into** a robot **before you know it**.

ROSEMARY: Well. I have a lot to do. Don't you have work to do?

FRANK: I did. but I **got** it **over with**, so I can leave early... Listen, it's my birthday.

ROSEMARY: Really? I didn't know! Happy birthday!

ローズマリー: もしもし?
　　フランク: やあ、ローズマリー。フランクだよ。元気?
ローズマリー: ええ、でも忙しいの。
　　フランク: 今日の午後映画に行く時間何とかなるかい?
ローズマリー: 行きたいんだけど、宿題がたくさんあるの。また今度ね。
　　フランク: いいだろ、少し休んじゃえよ。君はいつも勉強ばっかしてるじゃないか。いつの間にかロボットになっちゃうぞ。
ローズマリー: うーん、やることたくさんあるのよね。あなただって仕事あるでしょう?
　　フランク: あったけど片づけちゃったんだ。早く帰れるように... あのね、僕の誕生日なんだ。
ローズマリー: 本当に? 知らなかった! おめでとう!

D·I·A·L·O·G·U·E

FRANK: Thanks. I wanted to celebrate it with you.

ROSEMARY: Well, **when you put it that way**, how can I refuse? You **talked me into** it.

FRANK: Great. You don't know how glad I am that you **changed your mind**.

フランク: ありがとう。君と一緒にお祝いしたかったんだ。

ローズマリー: そうねえ、そんなふうに言われると断れないわよね。うまく口説かれちゃったわ。

フランク: やったね! 気が変わって本当に嬉しいよ。

➻ **7. I wish I could.** I wishの後は仮定法過去・過去完了がくる。
11. You're always studying! 進行形にすると感情がこもってくる。たとえばShe does very well at school. (成績が良い)は単に事実を述べているだけだが、She is doing very well at school. だと賞賛の気持ちが入ってくる。同様に、He is always forgetting things. (いつも忘れ物ばかりしている)とすると非難の感情が強く感じられる。

108 make (some) time to do ...
〜する時間を作る

A: I have to clean my house, do my laundry, make dinner, do my homework …
B: How are you going to **make time to** sleep?

A: 家の掃除、洗濯、夕食の支度、それに宿題もあるし…
B: それでよく寝るヒマがあるもんだよね。

❖ **make time for** *someone or something* 「〜のために時間を作る」

A: I'm sorry. The dentist is very busy today. Can you come in tomorrow?
B: Can't he **make some time for** me? I have a terrible toothache.

A: 申し訳ありません。先生は今とてもお忙しくて。明日来て頂けますか?
B: 何とかお時間を都合してもらえませんか? 歯がすごく痛むんです。

109 take a rain check
次の機会にまた誘う

A: Can you come over for dinner tonight?
B: I'm sorry, I can't. Can I **take a rain check**?

A: 今晩夕ご飯食べに来ない?
B: ごめんなさい。また今度誘って下さる?

A: Didn't they invite him to go swimming?
B: Uh-huh. But he has a cold, so he had to **take a rain check**.

A: 一緒に泳ぎに行こうって彼のこと誘わなかったの?
B: うん、でもカゼひいてて、またそのうちってことになったんだ。

❖ **give (*somebody*) a rain check** 「次の機会にまた誘う」

A: Can you come over for dinner tonight?
B: I'm sorry. I can't. Can you **give me a rain check** for next week?

A: 今晩家で夕食でもどうかしら?
B: ごめんなさいね、ちょっと無理なの。また来週誘って下さる?

➥ a rain checkはもともと雨で試合中止のとき渡す再発行入場券のこと。ここから招待に応じられなかったときの後日の招待という意味に用いられるようになった。

How About Going to a Movie?

110 take (time) off

休暇を取る

A: I need a vacation.
B: Why don't you **take** some **time off**?
A: I'll think about it.

A: 休みが欲しいな。
B: 休暇を取れば?
A: 考えてみようっと。

❖ take a break / coffee break 「休憩する」

A: I've been sitting at this desk for two hours. I need to **take a break**.
B: Me, too. Come on. It's time for our **coffee break**.

A: 2時間もずっと机に座りっぱなしよ。ちょっと休憩したいわ。
B: 僕もだよ。ねえ、ちょっとお茶でも飲んで休もうよ。

111 turn into *something*

(何か違うものに)変わる

A: What happened?
B: The milk in my refrigerator **turned into** ice.

A: どうしたの?
B: 冷蔵庫のミルクが凍っちゃった。

❖ turn *something* into *something* 「(何か違うものに)変える」

A: The cold weather **turned** the lake **into** an ice skating rink.
B: I hope warm weather will **turn** it **into** water again soon.

A: 寒さで湖がスケートリンクになっちゃった。
B: じき暖かくなってまたもと通りになる(氷が水になる)といいわね。

112 before one know it
いつのまにか、知らないうちに

A: Time is really flying.
B: It sure is. School will be over (finished) **before we know it**.

A: 時がたつのは本当に早いね。
B: まったくだよ。いつのまにか学校だって終わっちゃうよ。

A: Why are they so wet?
B: It started to rain. and **before they knew it**, they were walking in a foot of water.

A: あの人達なんであんなにびしょ濡れなの？
B: 雨が降り始めて、気がついてみたらまるで洪水みたいな中を歩いてたんだって。

➥ この表現を文頭、あるいは文の途中で用いるときはコンマ(,)をつける。

113 get *something* over with

かたずける

A: Some people say, "Don't do tomorrow what you can do today." I say, "Don't do today what you can do tomorrow."
B: I'm different. When I have something to do, like cleaning or work, I like to **get** it **over with.** Then I can relax.

A: 「今日できることを明日するな」っていう人もいるけど、僕は「明日できることを今日するな」っていう主義でね。
B: 僕は違うな。掃除や仕事みたいにすることがある時はまず片づけてしまえば後でゆっくりできるだろ。

➼ 「後でしなくてもいいように済ませてしまう」というニュアンス。買い物、料理、宿題、やっかいな会話、他人への訪問や電話など、気の進まない事がらに用いられることが多い。

114 when you put it that way

そういわれると

A: Your grades should be higher, Joe. I'm very disappointed in you.
B: Sorry, Dad. But I have three hours of soccer practice every day, and no time to study.
A: Make time to study. If your grades don't

A: おまえの成績、もっと良くてもいいはずだぞ、ジョー。がっかりだ。
B: ごめんね、お父さん。でもね、毎日3時間サッカーの練習があって勉強する時間がないんだよ。
A: 時間を割いて勉強しろ。成績が良くならなけりゃサッ

improve, you'll have to stop playing soccer.

B: When you put it that way, I guess I have no choice.

カーなんてやめろ。

B: そう言われちゃうと、もうやるしかないよね。

115 talk *someone* into *doing* ...
説得して〜させる

A: What are you doing here? I thought you were going to stay home.

B: Lisa **talked** me **into** com**ing**.

A: こんなとこで何してるの？家にいるのかと思った。

B: リサに来るよう**口説かれた**の。

❖ **talk *someone* out of *doing something*** 「説得して〜するのをやめさせる」

A: I thought you were going away this weekend.

B: I was going to go mountain climbing, but my brother **talked** me **out of** it because the weather is so bad.

A: この週末はどこかに出かけるんじゃなかったの？

B: 山登りに行こうかと思ってたんだけど、天候がひどいから兄さんに**やめるよう説得された**んだ。

▸▸ persuade someone (not) to do something よりも口語的な表現。

116 change one's mind(s)

気が変わる

A: What happened? We waited for you at the café.
B: I'm sorry. I was planning to join you, but I **changed my mind**. I went to the library instead.

A: Aren't you expecting friends?
B: They were supposed to arrive today, but they **changed their minds**. They're going to come tomorrow.

A: どうしたの？カフェであなたのこと待ってたのに。
B: ごめんなさい。ご一緒しようかと思ってたんだけど、ちょっと**気が変わって**図書館に行ったの。

A: お友達を待ってるんじゃないの？
B: 今日来るはずだったんだけど、**気が変わった**みたいなんだ。明日になるみたいだね。

➤➤ decide to do something else よりも口語的。

e·x·e·r·c·i·s·e·s

1 テープ(CD)を聴いて、次のダイアローグの空欄に適当な語句を書き入れてみましょう。

GODMOTHER: Cinderella, come here. I want to (1)_____ a beautiful princess so that you can go to the prince's ball.

CINDERELLA: Thanks, Fairy Godmother, but can I (2)_____? I have to (3a)_____ this cleaning (3b)_____ before my stepmother and stepsisters come home.

GODMOTHER: No, Cinderella! I won't (4)_____. (5)_____ fun! (6)_____ you'll be an old woman. Enjoy life while you're young. You're always working. (7)_____!

CINDERELLA: (8)_____, how can I refuse? OK, change me.

GODMOTHER: It took you a long time to (9)_____. OK. Stand straight and I'll wave my magic wand. ABRACADABRA!

CINDERELLA: Oh, Fairy Godmother! I'm so glad you (10)_____ going to the ball! Let's get going!

e·x·e·r·c·i·s·e·s

2. 次の1～9の文に対する返答として適当なものを153ページのa～iより選んでみましょう。

_____ 1. I have to work late tonight.
_____ 2. How'd you like to go to a concert tonight?
_____ 3. You can have the bike for half price.
_____ 4. What're you doing here? I thought you couldn't come.
_____ 5. You look great! Where have you been?
_____ 6. A month is a long time for a vacation.
_____ 7. Have you seen Bobby lately?
_____ 8. They're planning to go swimming where there are sharks.
_____ 9. Why do you look so happy?

a. I got my exams over with and I think I did pretty well.
b. Maybe. But before you know it, it will be over.
c. Again? But you promised to make time to be with the kids.
d. Yes. He's really turned into a nice young man, hasn't he?
e. You talked me into it. I'll take it.
f. They're crazy. We'd better talk them out of it.
g. I changed my mind when she told me it was free.
h. A lot of places. I took a month off to relax.
i. I'd really like to, but can you give me a rain check? I don't feel very well.

LESSON 8 **Answer Key**

Exercise 1

1. turn you into
2. take a rain check
3a. get   3b. over with
4. give you a rain check
5. Make some time for
6. Before you know it
7. Take some time off
8. When you put it that way
9. change your mind
10. talked me into

Exercise 2

| 1. c | 2. i | 3. e | 4. g | 5. h | 6. b |
| 7. d | 8. f | 9. a | | | |

Pulling an All-Nighter

徹夜で勉強する

Lesson 9

D·I·A·L·O·G·U·E

ALAN: Why do you look so tired?

ANNETTE: I **pulled an all-nighter** writing my report.

ALAN: Did you finish it?

ANNETTE: Yeah, just **in the nick of time**. I finished typing it a half hour ago, and I have to **turn it in** in five minutes. I'd better hurry.

ALAN: OK. See you later.

(*A few hours later*)

ANNETTE: Alan—I'**m** really **in hot water**. My teacher gave us a **pop quiz** and I couldn't remember anything. **My mind went** totally **blank**.

ALAN: Because you didn't **get any sleep**.

ANNETTE: That's right. And he read my report while I was **taking the quiz**. When the quiz **was over**, he asked to see me. He told me to **type** my report **over again** because it's such a mess.

アラン: そんな疲れた顔してどうしたの?

アネット: レポート書いてて徹夜よ。

アラン: 終わった?

アネット: ええ、最後の土壇場でね。30分前にタイプし終ってあと5分で提出しなきゃならないの。急がなくっちゃ。

アラン: あっそう。じゃまた。

(数時間後に)

アネット: アラン、本当に困っちゃった。先生に抜き打ちテストされて何も思い出せなかったの。頭の中もう真っ白。

アラン: 寝てないもんね。

アネット: そうなの。それに私がテスト受けてる間に先生レポート読んでたのよね、それで終わってから話があるって言うの。レポートの出来がひどいからやり直せって言われちゃった。明日提出しろですって。

D·I·A·L·O·G·U·E

He wants me to **hand it in** tomorrow.
ALAN: I think you'd better **take a nap** before you do any more work today.
ANNETTE: That's good advice, but I have another class at 2:00, and we're going to have a test.
ALAN: Another test? You sure **are under** a lot of **pressure**.
ANNETTE: **You can say that again.** I think I'd better go **hit the books** at the library because I don't want to **take the test cold**.
ALAN: You mean you didn't study for the test?
ANNETTE: How could I? I was writing my report!

アラン： 今日もうひと仕事する前にちょっと休んだほうがいいよ。

アネット： 本当にそうよね。でも2時にまた授業があってテストなの。

アラン： またテスト？そりゃ本当に大変だね。

アネット： あなたの言う通りよ。図書館で勉強したほうがいいみたいね。ぶっつけ本番ていうわけにもいかないし。

アラン： 準備してなかったの?

アネット： できるわけないでしょ、レポート書いてたのよ!

➻ **5. Yeah** Yes のくだけた形。
18. He told me to type tell A to do で「A に～するよう言う」の意味。
20. He wants me to hand it in want A to do で「A に～して欲しい」となる。
23. That's good advice advice は不可算名詞。数えるときは a piece of, a bit of を用いる。
26. You sure are 119ページの注を参照。

117 pull an all-nighter
徹夜で勉強する

A: I can't believe that the test is in only two weeks.
B: Neither can I. I'm going to study a little bit every night so I won't have to **pull an all-nighter** the night before the test.
A: So am I. I never do well if I don't sleep the night before.

A: テストまであと2週間なんて信じられない。
B: 同感だね。これから毎晩少しずつ勉強しておこう。直前になって**詰め込み勉強**しなくてすむようにね。
A: 僕も。前の晩に寝れないと決まって出来が悪いんだ。

➻ stay up は単に寝ないで起きていることで、理由は勉強に限らない。to burn the midnight oil は「夜中に(ランプの)油を燃やす」から転じて「夜遅くまで起きて仕事や勉強をする」の意味になるが、これは古めかしい表現なので聞いて分かればよい。

❖ **cram**「詰め込み勉強をする」

A: I'm sorry. I can't talk to you right now. I have to go **cram** for the history midterm. Have you started studying for it yet?
B: Uh-huh. I forced myself to start over the weekend.

A: ごめんなさい。今お話できないの。歴史の中間テストで**詰め込み勉強**しなくちゃ。あなたはもう始めた?
B: ええ、週末から無理やり始めたわ。

A: I wish I had done that. I have to read 150 pages and memorize all those dates. I'd better get started.

A: 私もそうすれば良かった。150ページも読んで日付なんかみんな覚えなきゃならないんだから。もう取りかからないとね。

➛ 「ただむやみに知識を詰め込む」という否定的なニュアンス。日本の塾や予備校を cram school と呼ぶことが多いが、この呼び方自体に否定的な価値判断が感じられる。

118 in the nick of time
最後の土壇場で

- We got here **in the nick of time**. The movie just started.
- You got here **in the nick of time**. We almost left without you.
- They got out of the house **in the nick of time**. The fire reached their house as soon as they were on the street.

ー私たちギリギリで着いたわね。映画ちょうど始まったところよ。
ー滑り込みセーフってところだね。君を置いてきぼりにして出かけようとしてたんだ。
ー彼ら**危機一髪**で家から外に出たんだ。通りに出たらすぐに家が燃え始めたんだよ。

➛ just in time, at the last (possible) moment よりもくだけた表現。

119 turn in …/hand in …

提出する

A: I'm so busy. I don't know what to do first.
B: What do you have to do?
A: I have to **turn in** two papers by next Tuesday.
B: I know how you feel. I just **handed** two **in** last week.

A: 忙しいの何のって。何から手をつけたらいいのかしら。
B: 何をしなきゃいけないわけ?
A: 来週の火曜までに小論文ふたつも**提出し**なくちゃいけないの。
B: 気持ち分かるよ。僕も先週ふたつ**出し**たばっかりだから。

➺ submit よりも口語的。

❖ hand out 「(テスト用紙などを)配る」

A: Please clear your desks. I'm ready to **hand** the quizzes **out**.
B: How much time will we have for the quiz?

A: 机に何も置かないで。テストを**配り**ますよ。
B: 時間はどのくらいですか。

➺ 新聞や牛乳を「配る」のは deliver を用いる。

❖ handout(s) 「ハンド・アウト、プリント」

A: What book are you using in your English class?
B: No book. The teacher gives us lots of **hand**-

A: 英語の授業ではどんな本を使ってるの?
B: 本は使ってないの。代わりに先生がたくさん**プリント**

outs instead. / を配るの。

❖ **hand back**「(テストや提出物などを)返す」

A: When will you **hand back** our tests?
B: I'll **hand** them **back** in a few days.

A: テストはいつ返してもらえるんですか？
B: 数日のうちに返します。

➻ return よりも口語的な表現。

120 be in hot water (with *someone*)
困っている、〜とごたごたを起こしている

A: What's wrong with her today? She looks so unhappy.
B: She's **in hot water with** her teacher because she cheated on her test.

A: あの子今日はどうしたの？とっても落ち込んでるみたいだけど。
B: 先生とまずいのよ。テストでカンニングしちゃったから。

➻ 「熱湯につかっている」が文字通りの意味。be in trouble (with someone) よりも口語的な表現。

Pulling an All-Nighter • 163

121 a pop quiz
抜き打ちテスト

A: Do you give **pop quizzes** in this class?
B: Yes, once in a while. I do that so you will study regularly, not just before tests.

A: この授業では**抜き打ちで**テストなんかあるんですか？
B: ときどきね。テストの直前だけじゃなく、いつもちゃんと勉強してもらいたいですからね。

➡ popはいきなりポンと出てくる感じ。ビックリ箱をイメージすると分かりやすい。quizは小規模なテストのこと。試験を表す語としては他にexamination, 略してexamがある。

122 my mind went (totally) blank
頭の中が真っ白になる

– At first, when I looked at the test, **my mind went blank**. So, to calm down, I closed my eyes for a minute or two. Then everything (the information that I had studied) **came back to me**.

ー最初テスト用紙を見たときは頭の中が真っ白になったの。だからね、気持ちを静めなきゃと思って、ちょっとのあいだ目を閉じてみたの。そしたらみんな(勉強したことが)思い出されてきて。

123 get (any/enough/a little/lot of) sleep

寝る

□□

A: Go to bed! If you **don't get any sleep**, you won't be able to get up in the morning.

B: I can't go to bed now. I have to read at least three more chapters.

A: もう寝なさい！**寝ない**と朝起きられないわよ。

B: まだ寝れないんだ。まだあと３章は読まないといけないんだ。

124 take a quiz/test

テストを受ける

□□

– Please don't make any noise. The students are **taking a test**.

– 静かにして下さい。学生が**テストを受けている**ところです。

➸「受験する」の意味でdo/make/receive a testは誤り。

125 be over

終わっている

- **A:** I'll do my homework when this show **is over**.
- **B:** No, you'll do your homework now! Turn off the TV.

- **A:** 番組が**終わったら**宿題をやるよ。
- **B:** ダメッ、今やりなさい! テレビは消して。

➡ 主語になれるものはa movie, a semester, a game, a partyなど。人間を主語にしてI'm over.というのは誤り。この場合はI'm finished.という。

126 type/do *something* over (again)

やり直す

- – I lost my homework. so I have to **do it over**.

- － 宿題なくしちゃった。だから**やり直さ**なきゃ。

➡ アメリカの大学では提出物はタイプするのが常識なのでtypeという語を使う。強調するときはtype/do something all over againとする。

127 take a nap

(少しの間)寝る

- **A:** What time is it?
- **B:** About 2:00, I think. Why?

- **A:** 何時?
- **B:** 2時くらいだと思うけど、どうして?

A: I think I'll **take a nap** for a half hour or so. I can't keep my eyes open.

A: 30分くらい**ひと寝入り**しようかと思って。もう目を開いていられないの。

128 be under pressure

気苦労がある

A: Modern women **are under** a lot of **pressure**. Many of them have to work, go to school, and take care of their families.
B: I like the old days when women just stayed home.
A: You're kidding. Really?

A: 現代の女性は色々と**気苦労が多くて**大変よね。働いて学校に行って、それに家族の面倒まで見なきゃいけないんですもの。
B: 女性が家庭におさまってた古き良き時代っていいわよね。
A: 冗談でしょ? 本気?

➜ 「圧力がかかっている」が文字通りの意味で、責任からストレス、緊張の高まっている状態をさす。

Pulling an All-Nighter

129 You can say that again!

本当にその通り

A: That test was really long.
B: **You can say that again!** I needed another hour.

A: あのテスト本当に設問がたくさんあったよね。
B: まったくその通りだよ。あと1時間は欲しかったね。

➥ 「それをもう一度言ってもいいよ」から相手の発言に全面的に賛成の意を表すために用いられる。

130 hit the books

勉強する

– Sorry I can't talk now. I have to **hit the books**.

― ごめんなさい、今お話できないの。勉強しなくちゃ。

➥ studyよりもずっとくだけた学生用語。

131 take a test cold
準備なしにテストを受ける

A: I can't believe I got an A!
B: Why?
A: I **took the test cold**.

A: Aがもらえたなんて信じらんない！
B: どうして？
A: テストぶっつけ本番だったから。

➜ これも学生用語。take a test without preparation よりもくだけた表現。

e·x·e·r·c·i·s·e·s

1 テープ(CD)を聴いて、次のダイアローグの空欄に適当な語句を書き入れてみましょう。

ALAN: What time is it?
CHARLIE: You don't want to know… It's 4:20.
ALAN: I need to (1)_____ .
CHARLIE: No you don't. Just get another cup of coffee.
ALAN: I wish I had (2)_____ every night. Then I wouldn't have to (3)_____ now. I still have a hundred pages to read.
CHARLIE: A hundred? We'd better stop talking. And I have to keep writing if I want to (4)_____ by 10:00.
ALAN: Let's take a five-minute break. I need to talk so I won't fall asleep… Don't you think that students today (5)_____?
We're each taking five classes and working in the bookstore and…
CHARLIE: So, what are you going to do? If you take fewer classes, it will take longer to graduate. Listen, I'd really like to talk, but I'm going to (6)_____ if I don't get this paper finished.
ALAN: OK. I'm going to (7)_____ . I'm setting my

alarm for 5:30. Wake me if I don't get up, OK? I'm not like you. I can't

(8)_____ like you can.

e·x·e·r·c·i·s·e·s

2 次の1～16の文に対する返答として適当なものを173ページのa～pより選んでみましょう。

_____ 1. Uh-oh! I forgot to pick her up from the airport.
_____ 2. I can't keep my eyes open.
_____ 3. Want to get some coffee when class is over?
_____ 4. If you don't hit the books a little more, you'll be sorry.
_____ 5. Can you do this over? I can't read it.
_____ 6. She's on vacation.
_____ 7. Ssh! The baby's taking a nap.
_____ 8. I've never taken a test cold.
_____ 9. Let's pull an all-nighter together.
_____ 10. English is a crazy language.
_____ 11. I was so nervous that my mind went blank.
_____ 12. You know, in some countries, people "do" a test.
_____ 13. I ran all the way. Am I late?
_____ 14. After I cram for a test, I forget everything I studied.
_____ 15. Take out a piece of paper for a pop quiz.
_____ 16. I'd like you to take out the handout I gave you yesterday.

a. That's good, because she's been under a lot of pressure.
b. Sorry. I didn't know.
c. There's always a first time.
d. Sorry. I need to sleep.
e. Oh no! Not again.
f. Boy, you're going to be in hot water when she sees you.
g. I can't find it. Can I have another one?
h. You can say that again!
i. Why don't you take a nap?
j. You're right. I'll try to work harder.
k. So do I. That's the problem with cramming.
l. For how long? The whole test?
m. No. You're lucky. You got here in the nick of time.
n. Sounds like a good idea.
o. Sure. I'll bring it in tomorrow.
p. I know. But in English it's "take."

LESSON 9 **Answer Key**

Exercise 1
1. get some sleep
2. hit the books
3. pull an all-nighter
4. hand this in
5. are under a lot of pressure
6. be in hot water
7. take a nap
8. pull an all-nighter

Exercise 2

1. f	2. i	3. n	4. j	5. o	6. a
7. b	8. c	9. d	10. h	11. l	12. p
13. m	14. k	15. e	16. g		

Sold Out

売り切れ

Lesson 10

D·I·A·L·O·G·U·E

CLAIRE: **That's not fair!** Why didn't they **let us know** earlier? We've been **standing in line** for nothing! **What a waste of time!**

PAUL: No, it isn't. We can still **get into** the 11 o'clock show.

CLAIRE: I don't know if I'll be able to **stay up** so late. The 11 o'clock show doesn't **get out** until about 2 A.M.

PAUL: Well, if I know you, you can stay up for THIS show. Come on. Let's stay in line and get our tickets. and then **figure out** how to **kill** the **three hours**.

クレール: そりゃないわよね! どうしてもっと早く言って
くれなかったのかしら? ずっと並んでてくたび
れ儲けなんて! すごい時間の無駄じゃない!

ポール: そうとも言えないよ。まだ11時からの上映には
入場できるんだし。

クレール: そんなに遅くまで起きていられるかしらね。11
時からのやつだと夜中の2時まで外に出れない
んだから。

ポール: あのね、君の好みからしてこの映画は起きてて
損はないと思うよ。さあさあ、並んで切符を買
っちゃおう。それから3時間をどうやってつぶ
すか考えようよ。

➻ 10. if I know you,「もしも僕が君のことを正しく理解しているとすれ
ば」がもとの意味。

132 be sold out

売り切れだ

A: Did you get tickets to the basketball game?
B: No. there were no tickets left. In fact, the tickets have **been sold out** for two weeks! (since last Sunday!)
A: So, did you try to get some for the soccer game instead?
B: No, but that's a good idea. I hope that **isn't sold out**, too.

A: バスケの試合の切符は手に入ったかい?
B: いいや、もう残ってなかったよ。2週間前から(先週の日曜から)**売り切れ**だってさ!
A: それじゃあサッカーの試合の切符は?買いに行ってみた?
B: いいや、でもそれいいかもね。また**売り切れでなきゃ**いいんだけど。

133 be on/for sale/will go on sale

発売中、発売予定

A: The newspaper says tickets for next week's football game **are on sale** now.
B: What are you waiting for? Let's go to the stadium right now. We can try to get tickets for next month's game, too.
A: No, those **won't go on sale** until Saturday.

A: 新聞で読んだんだけど、来週のフットボールの試合は**もう**切符**売ってる**ってさ。
B: これはぐずぐずしてらんないぞ。すぐスタジアムに行こうよ。来月ある試合の切符も買えるよ。
A: いや、それは土曜まで**発売されない**んだよ。

178 • Lesson 10

A: Look! Bill's house **is for sale**!
B: I didn't know that he wanted to move.

A: ごらん、ビルの家が**売りに出されてる**!
B: あの人が引っ越しするつもりだったなんて知らなかった。

❖ be on sale「特売で、セールで」

A: I think I'll buy that VCR that I saw last week.
B: Isn't it too expensive?
A: It was, but it**'s on sale** now. I can get it at half price.

A: 先週見つけたあのビデオデッキ、買おうかと思って。
B: すごく高いんじゃないの?
A: そうだったんだけど、いま**特売**なんだ。半額で買えるんだって。

➥「特売」の意味では on にも強勢を置く。

134 on a first-come, first-served basis
先着順で

A: Are the seats reserved?
B: No. Sorry. Seating is **on a first-come, first-served basis**.

A: 指定席ですか?
B: いいえ、申し訳ありませんが、座席は**先着順**ということになっています。

❖ first-come, first-served 「早い者勝ち」

A: OK, everyone. Dinner is ready. **First-come, first-served!**
B: Great! I'm starving.

A: よーし、みんな、夕食ができたわよ。**早い者勝ち**!
B: やったね! もうおなかが減って死にそう。

➥ こちらのほうがややくだけた表現。

Sold Out • 179

135 That's not fair!

不公平だ

- **A:** I'd like you to wash the dishes tonight.
- **B:** But I've washed the dishes every night this week. **That's not fair!**

- **A:** 今晩お皿洗ってほしいんだけど。
- **B:** でも今週は毎晩僕がやってるじゃない。**不公平じゃないか！**

- **A:** The test had a lot of words on it that we never studied.
- **B:** I know. **That** really **wasn't fair!**

- **A:** テストは習ってない単語がたくさん出てたよね。
- **B:** そうよね。いくらなんでも**あれはないわよね！**

136 let *someone* know

知らせる

- **A:** What time can you pick me up?
- **B:** I'm not sure. I'll **let** you **know** later.

- **A:** 何時ごろ迎えに来てくれる？
- **B:** まだよくわかんない。また**連絡するよ。**

- **A:** Good-bye. I'll miss you all.
- **B:** Write to us and **let** us **know** where you're staying.

- **A:** さよなら。みんなに会えなくなると寂しいよ。
- **B:** 手紙ちょうだい。どこにいるのか**知らせて**よ。

- **A:** Thanks for helping me move into my new

- **A:** 新しいアパートへの引っ越し、手伝ってくれてありが

180 • Lesson 10

apartment.
B: You're very welcome. **Let** me **know** if you need any more help.

B: お安いご用だよ。何かまた手伝えることがあったら**知**らせてね。

137 stand in line

列に並ぶ

A: I got to the bank early so I **wouldn't have to stand in line**. But look at all these people!
B: There are always lines here. I **stood in line** for half an hour last week.

A: 並ばなくてもいいようにって早く銀行に来たのに。この人たちを見てよ！
B: ここはいつでも並んでるのよ。先週私も30分**並んだ**の。

➼ stand on lineと言う人もいる。

Sold Out • 181

138 be a waste of *something*

〜の無駄だ

A: Standing in line **is a waste of** time.
B: Next time let's bring books to read while we're waiting.

A: 並んで待ってるのって時間の無駄だよね。
B: この次は待ってる間に読めるよう本を持ってこようよ。

❖ **waste (*something*) on (*something or someone*)**
「(お金や時間などを)(人や物に)無駄に使う」

A: Is that a good movie?
B: No, it's awful. Don't **waste** your money **on** it.

A: あの映画おもしろいかな？
B: いいや、ひどいよ。あんなのお金をドブに捨てるようなもんだ。

❖ waste time (*doing something*) 「～して時間を無駄にする」

A: I drove to work today and it took me two hours.
B: Why **waste time** driv**ing** in heavy traffic? You should take the train.

A: 今日ね、車で仕事に行ったら2時間かかったよ。
B: 混んでる中を車で通勤なんて時間の無駄じゃない。電車で行けばいいのに。

❖ waste (*something*) 「～を無駄にする」

A: I don't believe you're going to finish that huge sandwich!
B: I can't stand **to waste** food.

A: そんなばかでかいサンドイッチ、本当に食べきれるの？
B: 食べ物を無駄にするってできないんだ。

139 get into (a place)/get in

(学校や会場などに)許可されて入る

- **A:** I mailed my application. I hope I can **get into** the university.
- **B:** I know you'll be disappointed if you **don't get in**.

- **A:** 願書を送ったよ。大学、入学できるといいけど。
- **B:** 入れなかったらがっかりするだろうね。

❖ **get *someone* in/into**「(コネを使って)人を入れてあげる」

- **A:** We're going to have to stand in line for the opening of the art exhibit.
- **B:** I know the director of the museum. Maybe he can **get** us **in** (**into** the museum) early.

- **A:** 展覧会の開場、並ばないといけないだろうね。
- **B:** 美術館の館長さんと知り合いなんだ。もしかすると早く(美術館の)**中に入れて**くれるかも。

140 stay up

起きている

- **A:** You just woke up? It's noon!
- **B:** I **stayed up** late last night watching TV.

- **A:** いま起きたの？ もうお昼だよ！
- **B:** 昨日の晩テレビ見てて遅くまで**起きていた**んだ。

141 get out

下校する、退場する

A: Classes start at 9:00 and end at 3:00.
B: You mean we **won't get out** until 3:00?

A: 授業は9時に始まって3時に終わります。
B: それじゃ3時まで帰れないっていうことですか?

➻ 授業や映画などの後でその場所から「出ていく」こと。

❖ get out of (a place) 「～から外に出る」

A: Let's **get out of** the house for a while.
B: Good idea. I need some fresh air.

A: しばらく外に出ようか。
B: いいね。きれいな空気を吸わなくちゃ。

❖ get (*someone or something*) out of (a place)「(人や物を)～から外に出す」

A: Please **get** that dog **out of** here!
B: I'm **getting** him **out** right now.

A: その犬ここから追い出して!
B: 今そうしてる(連れ出している)ところだよ。

142 figure out

決める、理解する

A: We're having a lot of trouble with this project.
B: Let me help you **figure out** what to do.

A: この計画では本当に苦労するよ。
B: 何をしたらいいか**決める**の手伝うよ。

A: This is a really difficult problem. **I can't figure** it **out**. (= understand)
B: Neither can I. Let's ask the teacher to explain it to us.

A: これって本当に難しい問題だね。**わかんないや**。
B: 僕も。先生に説明してもらおう。

A: What? Joe sold his car last night?
B: Uh-huh. **I can't figure out** why he did it. (= understand)

A: 何だって？ジョーが車を昨日の晩売ったって？
B: うん。何でそんなことしたのか**理解に苦しむ**よ。

A: How do you like your new boss?
B: She's very moody. **I can't figure** her **out**. (= understand)

A: 新しい上司はどう？
B: とっても気分屋で、よく**わかんない**人だよ。

・・

➼ decide, understand などよりも口語的な表現。

143 kill (time) (by)

時間をつぶす

A: We're early. What should we do now?
B: We can **kill time by** playing cards.

A: 早く着いたね。何してようか。
B: トランプでもして**暇をつぶ**そうか。

A: Oh, no! The flight has been delayed.
B: Let's think of something to do to **kill the two hours**.

A: うわー、飛行機が遅れるんだって。
B: 2時間どうやってつぶすか考えよう。

❖ have (time) to kill 「時間をつぶす必要がある」

A: We **have two hours to kill.** What do you want to do?
B: Well, we can tell each other stories.

A: 2時間暇をつぶさなきゃ。何したい？
B: そうね、うわさ話でもしましょうか。

Sold Out • 187

e·x·e·r·c·i·s·e·s

1 テープ(CD)を聴いて、次のダイアローグの空欄に適当な語句を書き入れてみましょう。

DAN: How was the concert?
JEFF: We didn't (1)_____ .
DAN: You're kidding! I thought you (2)_____ for ten hours.
JEFF: We did, but the tickets (3)_____ before we got to the front of the line. It was awful. We (4)_____ ten hours standing in line.
DAN: Standing?
JEFF: Well, we did sit down for awhile. We (5)_____ by listening to music and sleeping.
DAN: Sleeping?
JEFF: Well, you know it was the middle of the night when we got there. I couldn't (6)_____ .
DAN: Did you have a sleeping bag?
JEFF: Yes. Luckily, I had just bought a really good one that (7)_____ for only $35.
DAN: That was lucky! Are you going to try to (8)_____ the next concert?
JEFF: Of course! Tickets will

188 • Lesson 10

(9)_____ on Saturday at 10:00 A.M., and I'm planning to be there starting Friday morning.

DAN: I can't (10)_____. Your're crazy!

JEFF: Maybe I am. But I love that music. And it's vacation now, so I (11)_____.

DAN: Are you sure you'll get tickets?

JEFF: I'd better! Tickets are sold (12)_____, and I plan to be the first one in line! Do you want to come to that concert with me?

DAN: Sure, if you stand in line for me.

JEFF: (13)_____! You have to stand in line with me. Come on! It's fun!

DAN: I'm not sure right now. I'll (14)_____.

Sold Out • 189

e·x·e·r·c·i·s·e·s

2. 次の1～18の文に対する返答として適当なものを191ページのa～rより選んでみましょう。

_____ 1. Uh-oh! They are sold out!

_____ 2. The tickets went on sale last week.

_____ 3. I bought this T-shirt for $40 on sale.

_____ 4. We'd better get to the theater early.

_____ 5. Those people are already being served.

_____ 6. Can you come over on Saturday night?

_____ 7. When will he find out if he got the job?

_____ 8. I hate standing in line.

_____ 9. My car was cheap, but it has no power.

_____ 10. Why aren't you studying? You're wasting time watching TV.

_____ 11. We're lost. We've been driving around in circles.

_____ 12. They couldn't get into the concert so they went out to dinner.

_____ 13. How late did you stay up on New Year's Eve?

_____ 14. Why won't she get out of bed?

_____ 15. How did he get out of jail?

_____ 16. I can't figure out how to use this computer.

_____ 17. He says one thing and does another. I can't figure him out.

_____ 18. We're early again. What should we do?

a. They'll let him know next week.
b. That's too bad. They missed a good show.
c. That's not fair! We were here first.
d. But I needed to take a break.
e. Check the manual.
f. I know what you mean. It's a waste of time.
g. Do you think it was a waste of money?
h. That's OK. We can get tickets for the next show.
i. And we're wasting gas, too.
j. He's not easy to understand.
k. And they're already sold out?
l. She says she has the flu.
m. I'm not sure yet. I'll let you know.
n. Good idea. Seating's first-come, first-served, isn't it?
o. His uncle got him out.
p. I guess we can kill time by playing a game of cards.
q. What a bargain!
r. All night long.

Lesson 10 Answer Key

Exercise 1
1. get in
2. stood in line
3. were sold out
4. wasted
5. killed time
6. stay up
7. was on sale
8. get into
9. go on sale
10. figure you out
11. have time to kill
12. first-come, first- served
13. That's not fair
14. let you know

Exercise 2

1. h	2. k	3. q	4. n	5. c	6. m
7. a	8. f	9. g	10. d	11. i	12. b
13. r	14. l	15. o	16. e	17. j	18. p

Don't Throw it Away—Recycle!

捨てないで。
リサイクル!

Lesson

11

D·I·A·L·O·G·U·E

DAVE: **Hold it**, Kathy! **What in the world** are you doing? **I can't believe my eyes!**

KATHY: What are you talking about?

DAVE: Don't you recycle? How can you **throw** glass **away**?

KATHY: Don't **get** so **upset**, Dave. I was only trying to …

LEE: She's right, Dave. **Take it easy**.

DAVE: OK, but I **can't get over you**. I thought you **cared about** the environment and…

KATHY: I *do* care, but there's no place to recycle bottles here, and I wanted to help **clean up**. You make me **feel** so **guilty**.

DAVE: I'm sorry. I did go a little crazy, but I **couldn't help it**. It's just that I've been **doing** some **research on** pollution, and I've **found out** that we're **running out of** places to put our garbage.

LEE: Listen, why don't we all **go through** these bags and **take** the bottles **out**. I'll

デイブ: ちょっと待って、キャッシー！ いったい何やってるの? 自分の目が信じられないよ。

キャッシー: 何言ってるの?

デイブ: リサイクルしないの? ガラスをそんなふうに捨てちゃうなんて。

キャッシー: そんな興奮しないでよ、デイブ。私はただ...

リー: 彼女の言うとおりだよ、デイブ。もっと気楽にいこうよ。

デイブ: わかったよ。でもちょっと信じられないね。君は環境のこともっと考えてる人かと思ったのに...

キャッシー: 考えてるわ。でもね、この辺りにはビンをリサイクルするところなんてないし、ただ片づけを手伝おうと思って。あなたにそんなに言われるとまるで自分が悪いことでもしてるみたいな気分だわ。

デイブ: ごめん。ちょっと言いすぎたよ。でもね、黙ってられなかったんだ。僕は公害の調査をしてるだろ、それでゴミを捨てる場所がだんだん足りなくなってきてるのが分かるからさ。

Don't Throw it Away—Recycle! • 195

D·I·A·L·O·G·U·E

take them home and recycle them.

DAVE: Are you sure it's no trouble? Because I can …

LEE: … no problem at all. They **pick up** newspaper, bottles, and cans **once a week** in my neighborhood. We've got a good recycling program.

KATHY: Well, let's **roll up our sleeves and get to work**.

DAVE: Ugh! What's in this bag???

リー: ねえ、僕らみんなでここにある袋を全部調べてビンを取り出そうよ。家に持ち帰ってリサイクルしようと思うんだ。

デイブ: 本当にいいのかい? 僕が...

リー: 大丈夫だって。僕の近所では新聞、空きビンや空きカンを週に一回集めてくれるんだ。いいリサイクル運動でしょ。

キャッシー: よーし、それじゃあ一丁仕事に取りかかりましょうか。

デイブ: うわっ、この袋何が入ってるの???

➼ **11. I *do* care,** これは強調の do。
12. help do で「〜するのに役立つ、〜するのを助ける」という意味。
14. I did go a little crazy, go + 形容詞で「〜になる」の意味。通常あまり好ましくない事がらに用いられる。*cf. go blind, go bad*
30. Ugh! 嫌悪・恐怖・軽蔑などの感情を表す。

144 Hold it!

待って

A: This refrigerator sure is heavy. Walk very slowly.
B: OK. Let's go.
A: **Hold it** for a second. I have to move my hand.
B: Are you OK now?
A: Yeah, ready!

A: この冷蔵庫、本当に重いぞ。ゆっくり歩いて。
B: よし、いこうか。
A: ちょっと**待って**。手を動かさなきゃ。
B: もういいかい。
A: うん、いいよ。

➵ 上の例にみられるように、せっぱ詰まった状況で用いられることが多いが、次の例のように、それほどでもないこともある。

– Hey, you guys. **Hold it**. We're coming, too.

– おーい、みんな**待って**くれよ。ぼくらも行くよ。

145 What in the world?/What on earth?

一体全体

A: **What in the world** are you doing here?
B: I came to surprise you on your birthday.

A: ここで**一体**何してるんだい?
B: 君の誕生日だから驚かしてやろうと思ってきたんだ。

A: **Where in the world** have you been? (*feelings: relief, anger*)
B: I'm sorry I'm so late and that I made you worry. I got stuck in traffic.

A: **一体**どこに行ってたの?
B: ずいぶん遅れて心配させちゃったね、ごめん。渋滞で身動き取れなくって。

- **What on earth** are you wearing? Those pants look fifty years old! (*surprise*)
- **Who on earth** could be calling us at 4:00 A.M.? (*surprise, anger, disbelief, fear*)
- **When on earth** will they get here? (*impatience, concern, anger*)
- **Why on earth** did they try to drive in this weather? (*concern. criticism*)
- **How on earth** can we get there by 8:00? It's already 7:30! (*concern, impatience*)

- 君ね、また何てものはいてるんだい？そのズボンまるで50年ぐらいたってるみたいだ。
- 朝っぱらの4時から電話してくるなんてどこのどいつだ？
- いつになればやって来るんだよ？
- よりにもよってこんな天気のときにどうして車なんかで行こうとしたの？
- **一体**どうやって8時までに行けるんだい？もう7時半だよ！

➛ 疑問詞と共に用いられて、驚きや怒りなどの強い感情を表す。

Don't Throw it Away—Recycle!

146 I can't believe my eyes!

我が目を疑うよ

A: **I can't believe my eyes!** Why did you dye your hair blond?
B: Relax. It's just a wig.

A: 我が目を疑うね！ なんで髪をブロンドに染めたりしたの？
B: たいしたことじゃないよ。カツラだってば。

❖ **I can't believe my ears.** 「耳を疑うよ」

A: **I can't believe my ears!** Six months ago, you couldn't speak a word of English. You've certainly learned a lot!
B: Thanks. I study a lot, and my roommate helps me.

A: 自分の耳が信じられないぐらいだよ！ 半年前はひと言も英語話せなかったのにね。本当に上達したよ。
B: ありがとう。ずいぶん勉強したんだよ。ルーム・メイトも手伝ってくれたし。

➨ 共に強い驚きを表す。

147 throw ... away/out

捨てる

A: Ugh! Smell this cheese.
B: It must be two months old. **Throw** it **away**.

A: うわっ、このチーズ、臭い嗅いでごらん。
B: もう2ヵ月ぐらいたってるね、これ。**捨てちゃえ**。

A: Where are my old jeans?
B: I **threw** them **out**.

A: 僕の古いジーパンはどこやった？
B: **捨てたわ**。

➻ 「ポイッと捨てる」という感じで、dispose of よりも口語的。

❖ get rid of *something* 「処分する、始末する」

A: I know that you want to **get rid of** those old clothes, but don't **throw** them **away**. Take them to a homeless shelter.
B: That's a great idea.

A: 君はこの古着を**始末しよう**と思ってるみたいだけど、**捨てちゃ**だめだよ。ホームレスの人達の避難所に持って行けば。
B: それがいいね。

➻ 捨てる場合にも他人にあげる場合にも用いられる。

Don't Throw it Away—Recycle!

148 get upset

気が動転する、気分を害する

A: Don't **get upset**. I told you that I'll come to the party. But I'll have to be a little late. I'll meet you there.
B: I don't want to meet you there. I want to go together.
A: You **get upset** so easily. This isn't such a big deal.

A: ガタガタ言うなよ。パーティには行くって言っただろ。ただちょっと遅れるだけだよ。あちらで会おう。
B: 向こうで会うんじゃなくて一緒に行きたいのよ。
A: すぐ怒るんだもんな、まったく。たいしたことじゃないのに。

❖ **be upset**「気が動転している、気分を害している」

A: I'm so **upset**.
B: What's wrong?
A: Everything was fine until I got my test back. I got a "C" and I thought I'd get an "A."

A: 頭に来たわ。
B: どうしたの？
A: テストを返してもらうまでは良かったんだけどね、C取っちゃったの。Aだと思ってたのに。

A: I have to tell you that I'**m upset with** you.

B: Oh, no. What did I do now?

A: You promised you'd clean up before I got home, and people are coming over in five minutes. This place looks terrible.

A: What **are** you **upset about**?

B: Do you really want to know?

A: I asked, didn't I?

B: Well, I'**m upset about** a few things at work. One thing is that they keep giving me too much work and I'm always behind. Another thing is...

A: 私ね、**怒ってる**のよ。

B: えー、僕何か悪いことしたかな？

A: 私が帰ってくる前に片づけておくって約束したでしょ。あと5分でお客さんが来るのよ。散らかってめちゃくちゃじゃないの。

A: 何がそんなに**不愉快**なの？

B: 本当に知りたいの？

A: だからきいてるんでしょ。

B: あのね、職場で**面白くない**ことがいくつかあるのよ。まずね、仕事が多すぎていつも間に合わないでしょ、それから...

Don't Throw it Away—Recycle!

149 Take it easy.
気楽に行く、くよくよしない、のんびりする

A: I have so much work to do. I don't know how I can ever do it. I have to get this all done by Thursday, and …
B: Take it easy. I'll help you. Tell me where to start.

A: What are you going to do on Sunday?
B: I'm just going to **take it easy**. I'll do some work in the garden and probably read for a while.

A: 仕事があんまりたくさんあって、どうやってこなせばいいのやら見当もつかないわ。木曜までに全部片づけなきゃいけないし、それに…
B: なんとかなるさ。手伝ってあげるよ。どこから始めればいいの？

A: 日曜は何してるの？
B: ちょっと**ゆっくりしようか**なと思って。庭いじりをして、たぶん少し読書するのも悪くないわよね。

➜ 命令形で別れ際のあいさつにも用いられる。

150 can't get over ...

信じられない

A: I just got back yesterday, and I'm leaving again tomorrow.
B: I **can't get over you**. You've become quite a traveler.

- I **can't get over** what she said to him. She let him know her feelings.
- I **can't get over** where they took us for dinner! It was so expensive.
- I **can't get over** when this work is due. We'll need at least another week to finish it.
- I **can't get over** why they got married. They don't love each other. They just want to live away from their families.
- I **can't get over** how much that costs. That's crazy. I won't buy it.

A: 昨日戻ったばかりなんだけど、明日また出発するよ。
B: **信じられない**や。本当にずいぶん旅行するようになったね。

— 彼女が彼に言ったこと、**ちょっと驚き**だよ。本当の気持ちを伝えたんだ。
— 私たちを夕食に連れて行ってくれたところ、**信じられる**？ とっても高いお店だったの。
— この仕事の締め切り、**ちょっとあんまり**だ。最低でもあと一週間はないと終わらないよ。
— あのふたり、**一体全体**どうして結婚なんてしたんだろう。愛し合ってなんかいないし、ただ家族と離れて暮らしたいっていうだけなんだから。
— あの値段、べらぼうだよ。ばかげてるね。僕は買わないで。

➟ can't believe よりも口語的な表現。

151 care about ...

〜を気にかける、心配する、〜に関心を持つ

A: He **cares about** his family, but he wants to leave home and get his own apartment.
B: Is there a problem?
A: Yeah. His family doesn't understand.

A: 彼は家族のことを**気にかけ ている**の。でも家を出て自分のアパートに住みたいと思ってるのよ。
B: 困ったことでもあるの?
A: ええ、みんな彼の気持ちを分かってくれないんですって。

A: Why didn't you give him some money? Don't you **care about** the homeless?
B: Sure I do. But I don't like giving money on the street.

A: なぜあの人にお金をあげなかったの? ホームレスの人達のこと、**考えてあげない**の?
B: そんなことないけど、道端で人にお金をあげるっていうのはしたくないの。

A: Do you **care about** politics? the environment? money?
B: No. I don't **care about** all that. I just care about music.

A: 政治に**関心ある**? 環境問題は? お金のことは?
B: そういうことはどうでもいいよ。僕は音楽にしか興味がないんだ。

➥ 「どうでもいい、ぜんぜん気にならない」という意味では I could/couldn't care less. とも言うが、かなりぶっきらぼうな言いかたなので注意を要する。

❖ **care for** *someone* 「(人を)気づかう、気にかける」
– He **cares for** his family,　— 彼は家族のことを**気にかけ**

206 • Lesson 11

but he wants to leave home and get his own apartment.

A: They **care for** each other, but they aren't ready to get married.
B: They're smart to wait.

ているの。でも家を出て自分のアパートに住みたいと思ってるのよ。

A: ふたりは互いに**好き合って**るけど、まだ結婚する気にはなれないみたい。
B: 待ってて正解よね。

→ care for はレストランなどで「〜はいかがですか」の意味で用いられることもある。次の例を参照すること。

A: Would you **care for** some more? (= Would you like ...?/ Do you want...?)
B: Thanks. Just a little.

A: もう少しいかがですか？
B: どうも。じゃ少しだけ。

❖ take care (of) 「世話をする、面倒を見る」

A: Can you **take care of** the baby for a few hours so we can go to a movie?
B: I'd be glad to. I hope he'll be awake so I can play with him.

A: 映画に行きたいんだけど、しばらく赤ちゃんの**面倒を見**てくれる？
B: よろこんで。起きててくれれば一緒に遊んであげられるんだけどな。

A: My car won't start and I don't know what to do.
B: Take it easy. I'll **take care of** it.

A: 私の車ちっともエンジンかからないわ。どうしよう？
B: 大丈夫。僕が**何とかして**あげるから。

A: Bye. I'll see you in a few weeks. **Take care** (of yourself).
B: I will. Bye.

A: じゃあ、2、3週間したらまたね。**体に気をつけてね**。
B: ええ、じゃあね。

152 clean up *something*

片づける

A: We can have a party in my house if everyone promises to help **clean up**.
B: Everyone? Men, too?
A: Uh-huh. Men, too.

A: Did you have any damage from the earthquake?
B: All the dishes fell out of the cabinets. It took us two weeks to **clean up** the kitchen. (*or*: clean the kitchen up.)

❖ clean「掃除する」

A: We **clean** (vacuum, dust, wash the kitchen and bathroom floor) every Saturday morning.
B: Every week? We clean only once a month.

A: みんな**お片づけ**手伝ってくれるなら私の家でパーティしてもいいけど。
B: みんなって、ぼくら男もかい？
A: そうよ、男性諸君もよ。

A: 地震で何か被害はあった？
B: お皿が食器棚から全部落ちちゃった。台所を**片づける**のに2週間もかかったんだから。

A: 毎週土曜の朝に**お掃除する**の。
B: 毎週？ 私のとこなんか月に一回だけよ。

153 feel guilty (about *something*)

ばつが悪い

A: My parents don't think that I write to them or call them enough. I didn't know that they felt that way and I **feel** kind of **guilty**.
B: Well, write to them more often and then you won't have to **feel guilty**.

A: 両親はね、僕がちゃんと手紙や電話で連絡してこないって思ってるみたいなんだ。そんなふうに思ってるとは気づかなくて、なんか、**悪いことでもしたみたいだな**あ。
B: それならもっとマメに手紙でも書けば。そうすればそんな**気まずい思い**しなくてもすむんじゃないかな。

A: I promised that I'd help her study on Sunday. I can't go to the beach.
B: Just tell her that you don't feel well.
A: I can't. I'd **feel** really **guilty about** lying.

A: あの子に日曜は勉強手伝ってあげるって約束したの。海には行けないわ。
B: 気分が悪いって言えばいいじゃない。
A: そんなことできない。ウソつくと**後味悪い**でしょう？

❖ **be guilty (of *something*)** 「～で有罪の、～の罪を犯した」

– She**'s guilty of** murder, but you can see from her face that she doesn't feel guilty.
– These two guys **are** not **guilty**, so stop asking them questions.

— 彼女は殺人で**有罪**になったけど、顔を見るとちっとも悪いって思っていないみたいだね。
このふたりの男たちは**有罪**ではありません。だからもう質問はやめて下さい。

Don't Throw it Away—Recycle!

154 can't help it/oneself/—ing ...
〜せずにはいられない

A: You're eating too fast.
B: I **can't help it**. I haven't eaten all day.

A: 食べるの早すぎるよ。
B: しょうがないよ。一日中何も食べてないんだ。

A: You're eating too fast.
B: I **can't help myself**. I haven't eaten all day.

同上

A: I **can't help going** shopping whenever there's a sale.
B: Neither can I.

A: 特売があるといつでも行かずにはいられないの。
B: 私も。

A: I **couldn't help telling** him what I really thought.
B: Is that why he's so upset?

A: 彼には私の本音を言わずにはいられなかったの。
B: それであんなに機嫌が悪いわけ？

210 • Lesson 11

155 do research on (*a subject*)
調査する、研究する

A: Let's go get some coffee.
B: I can't. I have to go to the library.
A: Didn't you go yesterday?
B: Yes, but I'm **doing research on** the assassination of John Kennedy and some of the books that I need can't be taken out of the library. So I have to work there.

A: コーヒーでも飲みに行こう。
B: いまだめなんだ。図書館に行かないと。
A: 昨日行ったんじゃなかったっけ？
B: うん、でもね、今ジョン・ケネディ暗殺について**研究してる**んだけど、必要な本で借り出しできないのがあって、あそこでやらないといけないんだ。

❖ **research**「調査する、研究する」

A: Excuse me. I'm **researching** what people do to improve their pronunciation. Can I ask you a few questions?
B: Sure.

A: ちょっとすみません。みなさんが発音を良くするためにどんなことをしているのか**調査している**んですが、ちょっと伺ってもよろしいですか？
B: どうぞ。

Don't Throw it Away—Recycle!

156 find out
(調べて)見つけ出す、分かる、知る

A: Have you seen my brother?
B: No. Why?
A: I have to **find out** what time (when) he's going to pick me up.

A: 私の兄貴みかけた?
B: いいえ。どうして?
A: 何時に迎えに来てくれるか**知りたくて**。

A: Where's the post office? I thought it was on this block.
B: So did I. Let's **find out** where it is.

A: 郵便局どこだっけ?この区画だと思ったんだけど。
B: 僕も。どこにあるか**探そう**よ。

....

➜ 目的語としては疑問詞で始まる句や節、that で始まる節や about で始まる前置詞句などが可能となる。次の例を参照すること。

- I need to **find out** who is doing research on John Kennedy.
- I'm trying to **find out** why he's been absent so long.
- Let's **find out** how to do this.
- When we **found out** that he was in the hospital, we called right away.
- We need to **find out** about it.
- We need to **find out**

― 誰がジョン・ケネデイの研究をしているか**知りたい**と思います。

― なぜ彼がこんなに長いこと休んでいるのか、**事情を調べている**ところです。

― このやり方を**調べよう**。

― 彼が入院中と**知って**、すぐにお見舞いに行きました。

― その件について**事実を知る**必要があります。

― 案内所がどこにあるか**見つ**

212 • Lesson 11

where the information desk is.	け出さなくちゃ。
A: Lisa's car was stolen last night. **B:** How did you **find** that **out**?	**A:** リサの車が昨日盗まれたの。 **B:** どうしてそんなこと知ってるの？

➦ find outは知識や情報について用いられる。「車のカギが見つからない」と言うときにI can't find out my car keys. は誤り。こういう場合はI can't find my car keys. とする。

157 run out (of *something*)

〜がなくなる

A: If we don't find a gas station soon, we're going to **run out of** gas. **B:** Why didn't you get gas before we left?	**A:** ガソリン・スタンドが見付からないと**ガス欠**になっちゃうよ。 **B:** 出かける前にどうして入れておかなかったの？
A: We're **running out of** milk. Can you go to the store? **B:** In a minute. Let me finish this first.	**A:** ミルクがもうなくなってきたね。お店に行ってきてくれる？ **B:** すぐ行ってくるけど、まずこれだけ食べちゃうね。
A: Where's Betty? **B:** We **ran out of** milk so she went to the store.	**A:** ベティはどうしたの？ **B:** ミルクが**切れた**からお店に行ったんだ。

Don't Throw it Away—Recycle!

158 go through *something*
～を調べる、検討する、くまなく探す

A: I can't find my paycheck.
B: Did you look in your wallet?
A: Three times. I **went through** everything, but my check wasn't there.

A: 給料の小切手が見当たらないんだ。
B: 財布の中は見たの？
A: 三度も見たよ。全部調べてみたけど、ないんだよね。

A: Look at this! When I was cleaning, I was **going through** some old photos and found this baby picture.
B: That's you? I can't believe it. You were really cute.

A: ちょっとこれ！お掃除のとき昔の写真を見てたらこの赤ちゃんの写真が出てきたの。
B: 君なの？信じらんないね。本当にかわいかったんだね。

➸ 目的語としては(警察が)houses, cars, files などや、(個人が) old clothes, old school notes, books, letters といったものが可能。

❖ go through 「(苦労などを)経験する」

– Many families are **going through** hard times because of unemployment.
– They **went through** a difficult divorce.

― 失業のため多くの家庭は**大変な思いをしている**。

― ふたりは大変な離婚を**経験しました**。

➸ experience よりも口語的。

159 take *something* out (of ...)
～を取り出す

A: Where are my keys? They were in my pocket a minute ago.
B: Maybe you **took** them **out of** your pocket when you were looking for change for the phone call.

A: カギはどこだったっけ。ついさっきまでポケットにあったのに。
B: 電話かけるとき小銭探してたでしょ、あのときポケットから出したんじゃないかな。

A: Hurry up! **Take** the letter **out of** the envelope! I can't wait.
B: Calm down. I'll **take** it **out**.

A: 早く！封筒から手紙出してよ！待ち切れないわ！
B: 落ち着いて。今出すから。

➼ かばん、引き出し、スーツ・ケース、ポケット、封筒など、閉じられた空間から「取り出す」ときに用いる。棚やテーブルから「取り出す」のはtake offを使う。

❖ take *someone* out (to)「～に連れて行く」

A: I'd really like to **take you out to** dinner for your birthday. Are you free Saturday night?
B: Oh, that's really nice. Thanks. I'm pretty sure I'm free.

A: 誕生日に君を夕食に連れて行けたらなって思うんだけど、土曜の夜は空いてる？
B: まあ、ステキ。ありがとう。もちろん空いてるわ。

➼ 「外に連れ出す」というのが文字通りの意味で、人を食事や映画などに誘って連れて行くこと。

Don't Throw it Away—Recycle!

160 pick up ...

～を受け取る、～を迎えに行く

A: I have to **pick up** my books at Sandra's house. and then I'll come home.
B: After you **pick** them **up**, could you stop at the store for some bread?

A: サンドラの家へ行って私の本を**返してもらうの**。それから帰るわ。
B: じゃその後(**受け取った後**)でお店に寄ってパン買ってきてくれるかしら。

A: Can you **pick me up** tomorrow if it rains?
B: Sure. No problem.

A: 明日雨だったら**迎えに来て**くれる?
B: もちろん、かまわないよ。

➺ 何かを「ヒョイとつまみあげる」という感じ。ここから何かを「受け取りに行く」、車で「迎えに行く」という意味になる。

161 once a week

週に一回

A: How often do you go to your art class?
B: Just **once a week**.

A: 美術教室はどれくらい行ってるの?
B: **週に一回**だけ。

➺ a は「～につき」の意味。また、二回以上は twice, three times, four times, ... となる。

162 roll up one's sleeves and get to work

取りかかる

A: You'd better stop reading the newspaper and **roll up your sleeves and get to work**. It's already one o'clock.
B: Just let me finish this article.

A: 新聞読むのなんかやめて**ひとつ仕事に取りかかった**ほうがいいよ。もう1時になるよ。
B: この記事だけ読んじゃうから。

➥➥ 「そでをまくりあげて仕事に取りかかる」が文字通りの意味で、体を動かす作業に用いられることが多い。日本人なら「手のひらにツバをかける」といった感じ。

e·x·e·r·c·i·s·e·s

1 テープ(CD)を聴いて、次のダイアローグの空欄に適当な語句を書き入れてみましょう。

ANITA: (1)_____ is happening to the earth? I (2)_____ .

PHILIP: What happened?

ANITA: There was another oil spill. There is oil covering miles of the ocean near the coast. I just (3)_____ how often this has happened. Isn't there anything they can do prevent this kind of thing?

PHILIP: I have no idea. But you shouldn't
(4)_____ .
(5)_____ !

ANITA: I (6)_____ . What kind of world will our children live in? The forests are being cut down, we have air and water pollution, we're (7)_____ places for our garbage. We need to (8)_____ the earth to make it a healthier place.

PHILIP: You're absolutely right. But if you (9)_____ the earth so much, why don't you do something about it?

ANITA: Are you trying to make me (10)_____ ?

218 • Lesson 11

PHILIP: No. I just think you should (11)_____ what you can do to help. Why don't you call one of the environmental groups?

e·x·e·r·c·i·s·e·s

2 次の**1**〜**18**の文に対する返答として適当なものを221ページの**a**〜**r**より選んでみましょう。

_____ 1. Hold it!

_____ 2. I don't know what I'm going to do. I'm so worried.

_____ 3. We've got a lot to do today.

_____ 4. How often do you brush your teeth?

_____ 5. What in the world is that?

_____ 6. Where's the bag that was on the table?

_____ 7. I can't get over how polluted the air is here. It smells terrible.

_____ 8. I feel guilty about driving. It adds to the air pollution.

_____ 9. I'm going to learn how to fly.

_____ 10. I lost my ring. I'm going to go through everything in my room 'til I find it.

_____ 11. Hey! Stop laughing!

_____ 12. What happened when you told them that you lost it?

_____ 13. I care about learning English, but sometimes I get a little lazy.

_____ 14. OK, everybody. It's time to clean up. Put everything away.

_____ 15. When should I take the cake out of the oven?

_____ 16. My pen ran out of ink.

_____ 17. I can't get over how beautiful your house is.

_____ 18. Would you care for some coffee, sir?

a. My pet snake.
b. I can't believe my ears!
c. Uh-oh—I threw it away. Was it important?
d. Take it easy. We'll find out what you should do.
e. Everything? Good luck!
f. They got really upset.
g. So let's roll up our sleeves and get to work. I'm ready.
h. Here's a pencil.
i. Twice a day. How about you?
j. Yes, de-caf (decaffeinated), please.
k. I know. On really bad days, older people and sick people are told to stay in their houses.
l. I know what you mean. It's hard work.
m. Where should I put the paint?
n. I'm sorry—I can't help it—you look so funny.
o. Why don't you ride your bike?
p. Thanks. We just painted it.
q. In about a half hour.
r. Do you want to come with us?

LESSON 11 **Answer Key**

Exercise 1
1. What in the world
2. can't believe my eyes
3. can't get over
4. get so upset
5. Take it easy
6. can't help it
7. running out of
8. clean up
9. care about
10. feel guilty
11. find out about

Exercise 2

1. r	2. d	3. g	4. i	5. a	6. c
7. k	8. o	9. b	10. e	11. n	12. f
13. l	14. m	15. q	16. h	17. p	18. j

Let's Make a Toast

乾杯しよう!

Lesson

12

D·I·A·L·O·G·U·E

HIROSHI: **Quiet down**, everyone. I'd like to **make a toast to** our class. **May you** all be healthy, happy, and successful in your lives. And successful with your English.

MARIA: **I'll drink to that!** And I'd like to make another toast. This one is to our teacher. Thank you for **bending over backwards** to explain this crazy language to us. You patiently **put up with** our questions, and we always knew that we could **count on** you to **give us a hand** when we needed help.

TEACHER: Thanks, everyone. And now I'd like to make a toast to you. I'll miss you, your questions, and your wonderful **sense of humor**. **I wish you the best,** and I hope that you'll all keep in touch with each other, and with me.

HIROSHI: We will, **no matter what**.

ヒロシ: お静かに、みなさん。ぼくらのクラスに乾杯したいと思います。皆さんが健康で幸福で、そして人生において成功されますように。そして英語の勉強も目標を達成されますように。

マリア: 賛成! それから他にも乾杯したいことがあるわ。私たちの先生よ。骨身を惜しまず私たちにこのとんでもない言語を教えて下さってありがとうございました。先生はわたしたちの質問に辛抱強く応じて下さいました。必要なときはいつでも助けていただけるって、先生のこと頼りにしてました。

先生: ありがとう、みなさん。さあ、今度は僕からみなさんに乾杯させて下さい。もう会えなくなって、みなさんの質問やすばらしいユーモアのセンスともこれでお別れかと思うとちょっと寂しい気がします。お元気で。これからもお互いに、そして僕ともご縁が続きますように。

ヒロシ: ぜひそうしましょう。

➻ 14. I'll miss you, miss は「人に会えなくなって寂しい、食べ物や習慣など、普段から慣れ親しんだものがなくて寂しい」という意味。
  17. you'll all keep in touch with each other, 「～と連絡を取りあう、つき合いを続ける」ということ。

Let's Make a Toast • 225

163 quiet down

お静かに

A: Can you help me get the attention of the audience?
B: Sure. **Quiet down**, please! We'd like to make an announcement.

A: みなさんにちょっと聞いて頂きたいことがあるんですが。
B: いいですよ。**お静かに、**みなさん！お知らせしたいことがあります。

➻ be quiet よりもていねい。

❖ **quiet (*someone*) down** 「静かにさせる」

A: The children are much too noisy. We can't begin.
B: I'm going to **quiet** them **down** so that we can start the show.

A: 子供さんたちがうるさくて始められないわ。
B: ショーが始められるように**静かにしてもらう**から。

164 make a toast (to)

乾杯する

A: I'd like to **make a toast**. We all wish you many years of happiness.
B: Thank you. And we'd like to **make a toast to** all our wonderful friends. Thank you for

A: **乾杯したい**と思います。これからも末永くお幸せに。
B: ありがとう。僕たちのすばらしい友達に**乾杯**。今日は僕達と一緒にお祝いしてくれてありがとう。

celebrating with us
today.

➻ make toastだと「トーストを焼く」の意味になってしまうので注意。

❖ Here's to *someone or something*「～に乾杯」

A: **Here's to** Mom and Dad. Happy anniversary!
B: This is such a wonderful surprise! Thank you.

A: お父さん、お母さんに**乾杯**。結婚記念日おめでとう！
B: これはびっくりしたわ。ありがとう。

A: **Here's to** success at your new job!
B: Thanks.

A: 新しい仕事でのご成功を**祈って乾杯**！
B: どうもありがとう。

❖ Cheers!「乾杯！」

A: I'm so glad we could get together for a drink.
B: So am I. **Cheers!**

A: こうして会って飲めるなんてとても嬉しいよ。
B: 私もよ。**乾杯**！

165 may you/we/they

～でありますように

□□

A: **May you** always be healthy and happy.

B: And **may we** always be friends.

A: 君がいつも健康でそして幸せでいられますように。

B: そして私たちがいつまでもお友達でいられますように。

166 I'll drink to that!

私もそれに乾杯!

□□

A: Here's to a great vacation!

B: **I'll drink to that!**

A: すばらしい休暇に乾杯!

B: 賛成!

➣ 人の乾杯に対して賛成の意を表す表現。

167 bend over backwards (to)
一生懸命努力する

A: Did you finish painting the house last weekend?
B: Yes, thanks to my brother. He **bent over backwards to** help us.

A: 週末に家のペンキ塗りしたんでしょ、終わった？
B: うん、弟のおかげでね。骨身を惜しまず手伝ってくれたんだ。

➺ 「後ろ向きに体を反らす」から「大変な努力をする」の意味になる。

168 put up with ...
〜を我慢する

A: How do you **put up with** your noisy roommates?
B: It's hard, but I like them a lot.

A: 君のにぎやかなルーム・メイト、よく我慢できるね。
B: 大変だけど、いいやつらなんだ。

A: I'm anxious to get back home. I can't **put up with** this cold weather.
B: Lucky you. I wish I were going with you.

A: 家に帰りたいよ。こんな寒い天気我慢できない。
B: いいなあ。僕も君と一緒に行けたらなあ。

➺ tolerate よりも口語的な表現。

Let's Make a Toast

169 count on ... (to)

～をあてにする

A: Thanks for giving me the chance to do this job. I hope I can do it well.
B: I know you can do it. And if you have any problems, you can **count on** me **to** help you.

A: この仕事をするチャンスをいただき、ありがとうございました。うまくできるといいんですが。
B: できるよ。もし何か困ったことがあったら私が**力になろう**。

A: What else do we need to pack for our trip?
B: We **can't count on** good weather, so we'd better take raincoats.

A: 旅行には他に何を持っていったらいいかな。
B: いつでもいい天気ってわけにもいかない(いい天気を**あてにできない**)だろうから、レイン・コートを持っていったほうがいいと思う。

➜ depend on よりも口語的な表現。

170 give *someone* a hand (with)
手伝う、助ける

A: Let me **give** you **a hand with** those suitcases.
B: Thanks. They're really heavy.

A: スーツ・ケース運ぶのお手伝いしましょう。
B: ありがとう。本当に重いの。

A: How did you carry all that?
B: My friend **gave** me **a hand**.

A: あれみんなどうやって運んだの?
B: 友達が手を貸してくれたの。

➥ help よりも「ちょっと手を貸す」という感じが出ている。なお、「賞賛する、拍手する」の意味でも用いられる。次の例を参照。

A: How was the jazz group at the Student Union?
B: Terrific! The audience **gave** them **a** big **hand**.

A: 学友会のジャズ・グループはどうだった?
B: 抜群!みんな大きな拍手してたよ。

Let's Make a Toast • 231

171 have a sense of humor

ユーモアのセンスがある

A: Did you have a good time with your old friend the other night?
B: Yes. I couldn't stop laughing. She **has** such **a** great **sense of humor**.

A: この間の晩、昔の友達と会って楽しかった？
B: ええ、笑いが止まらなかったわ。彼女のユーモア感覚、ピカーよ。

172 I wish you the best

ご幸運をお祈りします

A: **I wish you** all **the best**.
B: And I wish the same for you.

A: ご幸運をお祈りしています。
B: あなたもお達者で。

➼ 人に善意を伝えるためのあらたまった表現。

173 no matter what
何があっても

A: We're going to have a picnic Saturday, **no matter what**. I promise.
B: What if it rains?
A: Then we'll have the picnic on the porch.

A: 土曜はピクニックに行こう。絶対だ、約束する。
B: 雨だったら？
A: そしたらポーチのところでピクニックだ。

A: My plane doesn't get in until late. I'll wake you up when I get home.
B: **No matter what time you get here**, I'll be awake. I can't wait to see you!

A: 飛行機が遅くまで着かないんだ。帰ったら起こすよ。
B: 何時に帰ってきても起きてるわ。あなたに会うのが待ち遠しいわ！

❖ **What's the matter (with *someone or something*)?**
「どうしたの？」

A: **What's the matter** (with you)? Don't you feel well?
B: I'm so tired, and I still haven't finished my homework.

A: どうしたの？気分が良くないの？
B: とっても疲れてるの。宿題もまだ終わってないし。

❖ **It doesn't matter.** 「かまわないよ」

A: I'm sorry I'm late.
B: **It doesn't matter** because we still have time to get there.

A: 遅れてごめんなさい。
B: いいのよ。まだ向こうへ行く時間はあるから。

Let's Make a Toast • 233

e·x·e·r·c·i·s·e·s

1 テープ(CD)を聴いて、次のダイアローグの空欄に適当な語句を書き入れてみましょう。

ASTRONAUT 1: (1)_____, everyone. It's time to (2)_____ to ourselves. We've now been up here in space for 100 day.
(3)_____ be up here for another 100!

ASTRONAUT 2: (4)_____!

ASTRONAUT 3: I won't! I can't (5)_____ this life any more. I want to go home.

ASTRONAUT 2: Why? (6)_____? Are you homesick? We have all (7)_____ to make you happy here. You have the best bed, good books to read,…

ASTRONAUT 3: I know it, and I thank you. But I'm going to go back home soon, (8)_____.

ASTRONAUT 1: How are you going to get there?

ASTRONAUT 3: With the supply ship. The guy on the supply ship told me that I could go with him next time if I (9)_____ with his

	work.
ASTRONAUT 1:	When did he say he would be here again?
ASTRONAUT 3:	In two weeks.
ASTRONAUT 1:	Ha! Two weeks? He probably won't be back for two months!
ASTRONAUT 3:	That's not very funny!
ASTRONAUT 1:	You have no (10)_____ .
ASTRONAUT 3:	I know he'll be here in two weeks. That's what he told me, and I am (11)_____ him to come.
ASTRONAUT 2:	And if he doesn't, what will you do?

e·x·e·r·c·i·s·e·s

2 次の 1 ～ 12 の文に対する返答として適当なものを 237 ページの **a** ～ **l** より選んでみましょう。

_____ 1. I'd like to make a toast to the new graduate. May she never have trouble finding a job!

_____ 2. Please quiet down.

_____ 3. I can't hear the TV because the kids are making so much noise.

_____ 4. Great speech! Let's give her a big hand!

_____ 5. Why are you so upset?

_____ 6. It's so hot here all the time. Do you like it?

_____ 7. Why did she leave so early?

_____ 8. You'll help me with my homework tonight, won't you?

_____ 9. Where are you going?

_____ 10. Can I give you a hand?

_____ 11. The jokes in that movie weren't so funny. Why were you laughing so much?

_____ 12. Bye, Chris. Have a good trip. I wish you the best. And remember to write.

a. Thanks, I really appreciate it.
b. She couldn't put up with the noise.
c. I will, no matter what.
d. I'll drink to that.
e. Not really, but I put up with it.
f. Sorry. I didn't realize we were being so noisy.
g. Bravo, Cindy! You did a great job!
h. I guess I have a strange sense of humor.
i. I'll try to quiet them down.
j. I bent over backwards to help them, but they didn't even thank me.
k. You can count on me.
l. To give them a hand with their homework.

Lesson 12 Answer Key

Exercise 1
1. Quiet down
2. make a toast
3. May we
4. I'll drink to that
5. put up with
6. What's the matter
7. bent over backwards
8. no matter what
9. gave him a hand
10. sense of humor
11. counting on

Exercise 2
1. d	2. f	3. i	4. g	5. j	6. e
7. b	8. k *or* c	9. l	10. a	11. h	12. c *or* k

I·N·D·E·X

A

about to, be 48
all day (long) 64
all night (long) 64

B

before one know it..............147
bend over backwards..........229
bookworm, be a 93
break a promise 132

C

can/can't afford 6
can/can't tell 9
can't get over 205
can't help 210
can't stand 107
can't stop................................65
care about 206
care for 206
catch a cold 62
chances are 67
change one's mind(s) 150
chicken, be 15
chicken, be a 15
clean......................................208
clean up................................208
come on..................................25
couch potato, a 90

count on 230
cram.......................................160
cut in line 120
cut out 14

D

deep down................................8
do over 166
do research on.....................211
do something (by) oneself....47
do something on one's own.47
don't be silly 49
don't be so hard on 126
drop by...................................26
drop in....................................26
drop in at 26
drop in on 26
drop off 27
drop out 27
drop out of.............................27
dropout (be a) 27
dying of hunger, be 13
dying of thirst, be 13
dying to, be............................13

E

eat out...................................122
end up 133

F

feel free	28
feel guilty	209
feel like	85
feel sorry for	70
figure	129
figure out	186
find out	212
first-come, first-served	179
for ages	24
for good	11
for here or to go	122
for sale, be	178
freeze	46

G

get back in touch	29
get cold feet	6
get going	26
get in	184
get in line	120
get in touch again	29
get into	184
get involved in	94
get married	9
get out	185
get over	68
get over with	148
get rid of	201
get sleep	165
get together	82
get tongue-tied	46
get up the nerve	45
get upset	202
give a rain check	145
give someone a hand	231
give up	132
glued to the TV/tube, be	91
go cold turkey	126
go out of one's mind	42
go out to eat	122
go through	214
going on, be	44
good for you	48
guilty, be	209

H

hand back	163
hand in	162
hand out	162
handout	162
hang up	42
hang up on	43
have a cold	62
have a fever	66
have a long way to go	131
have a lot/nothing in common	14
have a seat	49
have a sense of humor	232

have cold feet 6
have fever 66
have second thoughts 7
have something on one's mind 103
have time to kill 187
here goes 51
here you go 88
here's to 227
history repeats itself 12
hit pause/play 89
hit the books 168
hold it 198
how about 84
how's it going 130
hurt someone's feelings 102

I

I can't believe my ears 200
I can't believe my eyes 200
I have news for you 62
I know what you mean 65
I wish you the best 232
in ages 24
in good/bad shape, be 69
in hot water, be 163
in one's way, be 25
in the mood, be 83
in the nick of time 161
in the same boat, be 63
in the way, be 25
in touch, be 29
involved in, be 94
involved with someone, be .. 94
it doesn't matter 233
it's about time 125
it's my turn 121
I'll drink to that 228

K

keep a promise 132
keep in touch 29
keep someone company 64
kidding, be 87
kill time 187

L

let someone know 180
let's go Dutch 121
let's split it 121
let's split the check 121
let's split the tab 121
look who's here 128
lose touch 29

M

make a promise 132
make a toast 226
make oneself at home 82
make oneself comfortable 82
make time 144

make up 104
married, be 9
may you/we/they 228
move over..................................88
my mind went blank...........164

N

no matter what.....................233

O

on a first-come, first-served basis...................................179
(it's) on me............................120
on one's way, be 24
on sale, be 178
on someone's mind, be 102
on the way, be........................24
once a week 216
out of one's mind, be 42
out of one's way, be 25
out of touch, be 29
over, be..................................166

P

pain in the neck, a..................41
pain, a...40
pick up 27
pick up 216
please leave a message after (you hear) the beep 40
pop quiz, a............................164

pull an all-nighter................160
put (a book) down.................93
put up with............................229

Q

quiet down 226
quit cold turkey 126

R

read someone's mind............10
research..................................211
roll up one's sleeves and get to work 217
run into 30
run out....................................213

S

scare someone out of his/her wits 86
scared out of one's wits, be ..86
scared to death, be.................86
shoot..11
show up 106
so far..130
so far, so good 131
sold out, be 178
sound like 66
speak of the devil 128
spend time...............................91
stand for................................106
stand in line..........................181

stand someone up	103
stand still	44
stay in touch	29
stay up	184
stood up, be	103
stop by	26

T

take (time) off	146
take a break	146
take a class	124
take a coffee break	146
take a deep breath	50
take a nap	166
take a quiz/test	165
take a rain check	145
take a test	124
take a test cold	169
take care	207
take it easy	204
take out	215
take someone's temperature	66
take turns	121
talk someone into	149
talk someone out of	149
tearjerker, a	84
that makes two of us	86
that's final	122
that's funny	92
that's not fair	180
that's that	122
through, be	12
throw away	201
throw out	201
to be honest with you	102
to tell you the truth	102
tongue-tied, be	47
treat someone	105
turn in	162
turn into	146
type over	166

U

under pressure, be	167
up to, be	123
upset, be	202

W

waste of, be a	182
waste on	182
waste time	183
what do you mean	65
what in the world	198
what on earth	198
what's up	123
what's the matter	233
when you put it that way	148
why do you ask	90
will go on sale	178
wind up	16

wish me luck 50
work out 104
write down 43

Y

you can say that again 168
you('ve) got me 124
you're pulling my leg 87
you've got a point (there)...107

<訳者略歴>

柳浦　恭

上智大学大学院修了(応用言語学)。千葉経済大学短期大学部商経科助教授。共著に『TOEFL受験マニュアル』(秀英書房、グラマー・ボキャブラリー担当)がある。

耳できいて、使える
最強英語イディオム・ハンドブック

2003年5月10日　初版発行

著　者　Helen Kalkstein Fragiadakis
訳　者　柳浦　恭
発行者　森　信久
発行所　株式会社　松柏社／トムソン・ラーニング
発売所　株式会社　松柏社
　　　　〒102-0072　東京都千代田区飯田橋1-6-1
　　　　TEL　03 (3230) 4813（代表）
　　　　FAX　03 (3230) 4857
　　　　e-mail: info@shohakusha.com
　　　　http://www.shohakusha.com

カバーデザイン／小島トシノブ
印刷・製本／（株）平河工業社

ISBN4-7754-0042-8

略号＝6027

※本書は好評を博してまいりました『アメリカン・カレッジ・イディオム』を、音声ＣＤ付とし、タイトル、表紙デザインを一新して改めて発売したものです。